W9-BLD-309

STEWART BRONFELD

# Writing
# for Film
# and
# Television

A TOUCHSTONE BOOK
*Published by Simon & Schuster, Inc.*
NEW YORK

To Beverly, with love

Copyright © 1981 by Stewart Bronfeld

All rights reserved
including the right of reproduction
in whole or in part in any form

First Touchstone Edition, 1986

Published by Simon & Schuster, Inc.
Simon & Schuster Building
Rockefeller Center
1230 Avenue of the Americas
New York, New York 10020

Originally published by Prentice-Hall, Inc.

TOUCHSTONE and colophon are registered trademarks of
Simon & Schuster, Inc.

Manufactured in the United States of America

10 9 8 7 6 5 4 3 2    Pbk.

Library of Congress Cataloging-in-Publication Data

Bronfeld, Stewart.
   Writing for film and television.

   (A Touchstone book)
   Reprint. Originally published: Englewood
Cliffs, N.J. : Prentice-Hall, c1981.
   Includes index.
   1. Moving-picture authorship.  2. Television
authorship.  I. Title.
PN1996.B73   1986        808'.066791        86-15538
ISBN 0-671-62828-3 Pbk.

STEWART BRONFELD was a staff producer-writer for the NBC Television Network for more than sixteen years. In addition to producing he has written many network television programs, as well as films released by Columbia Pictures and Universal Pictures. His work has won two International Broadcasting Awards from the Hollywood Radio and Television Society and an Emmy Award nomination.

Mr. Bronfeld is the author of two other books, *How to Produce a Film* and *Careers in Television*. He has taught motion picture and television scriptwriting at Yale University.

# Contents

CONTENTS vii

The TV game show.
Soap operas.
Documentaries.
Miscellaneous television writing.

Afterword                                      138
Index                                          139

# Foreword

I am a tremendous admirer of creative writers. I respect them. I feel that I work well with them. And while I have upon occasion rewritten dialogue and scenes, and while a kind of rewriting takes place on the set every day, I account myself an interpreter, conveying into a new form the original concept of the author.

Production for the stage or screen is a collaborative affair of the highest order. I am not a great believer in the so-called "Auteur" theory of film making except in the rarest of circumstances, the work of a Charles Chaplin for instance. But I am a firm believer in the old saying that film is the director's medium. The director is, and must be, the person in charge of the set (and of post-production work), responsible for all the creative work of actors, staff and crew in interpreting on the screen (faithfully, it is hoped) the work of the writer. Failure at this point has led many writers to want to direct in order to protect their material or to put their image of their writing on the screen more accurately, free of distortion. It is for the same self-protective reason that many directors become their own producers: control of the final version of the film.

The ideal situation, not always obtained, occurs when there is total understanding and creative togetherness between writer, director and producer. This does not necessarily mean one person wearing all three hats, for this person (except for that rarest genius) is in gravest danger of loss of that objectivity which separately functioning individuals, working harmoniously together, can achieve.

Those of us who were lucky enough to obtain our early professional training in the pressure cooker that was live television (New York, circa 1949–1959) experienced this collaboration at its best. The writers were given the golden opportunity to be a major partner in the production of their scripts, to attend all rehearsals, to be able to see for themselves what needed to be changed to make a scene play and a script work or to accommodate the physical limitations of the studio, to be forced to rewrite under extreme pressure of time, to edit and cut for length—in short, to learn their craft the hard way and the best way: by doing.

The film writer, unlike the writer of those early live television dramas, is always long gone and unavailable when those crises arise on the set which make changes of scene, structure and dialogue necessary. The writer is thus at the mercy of the taste and creativity of the director and actors, and can but hope for the best.

The way I have found to minimize this problem is to be able to hold pre-shooting rehearsals. Even two or three days sitting around a table with the actors reading the script aloud, getting acquainted and accustomed to each other, discussing the characters and situations, are invaluable to director and writer. In these quiet and less-pressured circumstances, relationships can be explored, scenes and lines that don't work can be rewritten, length, pace and timings can be discussed, ideas for staging can be expressed. It is an incredible timesaver later on the set and an opportunity to involve the writer in the production as far as the mechanics of film making will allow.

True, there are those times when it is better that such work take place just between actors and director, if the problems are such that they can best be resolved by them alone. However, too many such situations might indicate that the director is doing the wrong scripts or should be writing his or her own.

In my view, the quality of writing for television specials

is every bit as good as any other dramatic writing, often better, because in recent years increasing costs and higher risks have so often caused theatrical films to rely on spectacle and plot at the expense of character and dramatic reality. As a result I have many times found more satisfaction in what I have done and have been more moved by what I have seen on the television screen than in a theatre, mired in popcorn, chewing gum and noisy audiences. (The problem lies in the violence so often done to the mood and style of a drama by insensitive, gross and jarring commercials. That is an entirely different subject, and one on which whole volumes could be written.)

This book works on the assumption that the new and inexperienced script writer has something worthwhile to say, that his or her story is worth telling. The search for good scripts, for new, fresh, interesting material is endless and frustrating. Over a good many years I have tried conscientiously to read and respond to hundreds of unsolicited scripts, outlines and story ideas submitted by new and aspiring writers.

As I pick up a new script and warily begin to read, I know that if it has characters and conflicts which are interesting, dialogue which flows and has reality, action which is compelling, and/or a style of storytelling that takes hold of the imagination, its form and style are of secondary importance. Nevertheless, I do recognize that, like it or not, my subconscious recognition that this new script is from the hand of a totally inexperienced writer works against my receptiveness to it. That is quite unfair to the new Tennessee Williams who is eagerly awaiting that first recognition, but it is a fact. A script which labels itself "amateur writer" has the proverbial two strikes on it before the battle begins, to mix a metaphor or two. It is simply that if I see a script which identifies itself as "professional," I know that I have a much better chance of finding something good and worthwhile than if it is clearly the work of an amateur or a beginner.

Therefore, Mr. Bronfeld is correct in his emphasis on form (and his reasons why this particular form or structure is important) in this handbook for new script writers. It was only when

I read what he has to say that I realized how much one tends to prejudge a script negatively if it lacks the proper form.

I also say "Amen" to Mr. Bronfeld's strictures against over-coaching of actors by writers who indicate too specifically just how the writer conceives the lines being played. It is one of the first things I take a blue pencil to, while trying to be judicious in leaving those which are truly significant to the writer's intent. Overexplicitness of this kind is not only unhelpful, it can often be a burden and a danger if not strictly ignored, which is some-times very hard for actors to do when they, too, are bent upon trying to convey the author's wishes.

On the other hand, when an author overwrites the staging and camera instructions, I do read and digest it all, trying to gain as much insight into his or her vision as possible. If it is overexplicit I usually also give this the blue pencil treatment when preparing the final versions of the script for actors and production staff. Even then, however, I find that on the set I often tend to ignore the script's camera and staging specifics, sometimes without really meaning to do so. At times the moves come out as the writer had envisioned, at times they don't. In short, I agree with Mr. Bronfeld: the doing, ultimately, must be left to the director and the actors.

Finally, while I have always dedicated myself to interpreting faithfully what the writer has conceived, I often allow the actor to change specific words if it helps him or her to convey the emotion more fully, more truthfully, more believably, and when I feel it will not change or distort the intent. When you are dealing with Shakespeare, Tennessee Williams, Paddy Chayev-sky or Loring Mandel, however, you change at your peril. The first two I have never worked with, although I have done their works. The latter two are examples of artists who have a specific reason for every word. They will change and rewrite when nec-essary, but the words are always specifically chosen for a very well thought out reason.

This book is filled with sound, practical advice for the beginning script writer. I am in general and specific agreement with almost everything the author says. Writing may look easy.

Writing professionally is anything but easy. I salute those who do it well.

I commend this book to those for whom it is intended, asking new writers to absorb it first, then write your script. The results will be better for us all. For that, thanks, Stewart.

Delbert Mann

Los Angeles

# Preface

This book is for someone who has typewriter and paper at hand and wants to be able to use them to write a motion picture or television script as soon as possible. Preferably a good one.

It is therefore a "how to" book, clearly meant to be *used*—but it strives to make the "how" more meaningful by always explaining the "why." The more a writer understands about the chain reaction of production activity set off by the script on its way to the screen, the better that script will be.

Every part of the book reflects how the script writer relates to the everyday working world of the profession. Knowing what really happens out there is as important in the education of a script writer as learning about dialogue, scene construction or camera angles.

The writing of scripts is a profession, but the selling of scripts is a business. No book about writing for film and television could possibly be complete without fully covering the subject of script markets, and how to sell to them—for unless a script is sold, it is not produced, which to me means it is not yet in its final form.

This book is not about how to write scripts, but how to write good scripts. What makes one screenplay or teleplay better written than another is no mystery. As you will see, the factors that make the difference can be identified and explained. The skill with which they are applied, however, is what talent is all about. That part is up to you.

S. B.

# 1
# The Myth
# Versus the Reality

The beginning teleplay or screenplay writer is about to enter a world he or she may know little about except for legends and fables about glamour and big money—all of which are true. But just as true of that world can be disappointment and financial uncertainty, for wherever the rewards are great the competition is fierce. Therefore, just as important as knowing how to write a script is knowing the realities of the movie and television industries as they are today.

In the thirties and forties the movie industry was "Hollywood," and in that district of Los Angeles the major studios were giant factories producing movies at the rate of one a week at their busiest. Like any factory geared to mass-produce a product, the movie studio had a huge roster of salaried employees, from makeup experts to famous stars. Script writers were often on a weekly salary and, like every other worker in the factory, were expected to keep their output flowing. The quality of the movies varied from awful to memorable, but going to the movies was such a regular habit that the constant stream of films had a ready market. Some factories specialized in the "B-movie," a lower-budget, less pretentious picture which traditionally was paired with an "A-movie" each week at local theatres.

Today there is no Hollywood in the old terms of movie production. Those big studios which have not been torn down now provide facilities for transient television production companies and for any independent movie producers who don't happen to be shooting in Spain or Italy. The movie business conducted by these studios today is primarily the financing and distribution of pictures which somebody else makes.

What happened to the movie industry, of course, was television, which has replaced the B-movie in the viewing habits of the general public. Today every theatre movie is an A-movie; but fewer of them are produced, and they cost more to make as well as to go and see. These fewer, more expensive movies are the key factor in the structure of the movie business as it has evolved. Now each picture is a separate project, individually financed, produced and distributed.

To the script writer, this all means that the market has shrunk and so the stakes are higher on each projected movie. It also means that, far from the days of "grind 'em out fast," there is a demand for higher quality in the writing of each script. Where most films of yesterday got lost in the fast shuffle of the weekly change of bill at the neighborhood movie house, today's film stands out in the sharp focus of "showcasing" at a smaller number of selected theatres. With higher and higher admission prices, people no longer go to the movies as a regular habit; they go to see a specific film. Knowing this, the people with the power to say yes or no to a script look for the very best one their money can buy—whether that means from an Oscar-winner getting $400,000 or from a newcomer getting the low-budget screen minimum.

While it is not easy to make that crucial first sale in either movies or television, the very fact that television consumes scripts in such incredible quantities means that it is more likely to offer entry to the new script writer. But while the entry is comparatively easier, the landscape is comparatively more exotic.

To truly understand television, you first must unlearn a popular misconception. Except in the strictest technological sense, *television is not primarily a communications medium.* It is primarily a *sales medium.* In an interesting reversal of the normal box office concept, *it sells its audience* to its actual and only customers, the advertisers. The presentation of programs is not what the business is all about, for the programs are merely the packages for the commercials which alone bring in the profits and pay everyone's salary.

This explains a fact of life known to anyone working in television: the higher executive positions at a network or a station more often are held by people who worked their way up through the sales department, not through the program staff. Consequently, the people who decide what goes on the air generally are sales experts, not communications experts.

But most significant to script writers and to the producers who buy their work, television is geared to a mass market—and a merchant selling only to a mass market must appeal to the broadest possible base of tastes. This explains what you see on any network or local station during a typical evening of television.

The industry is big, and also incredibly pervasive; a recent census shows that more than 98 percent of American families own at least one TV set—more families than have kitchen ranges or refrigerators. In terms of money coming into its cash register television is even more impressive. Remember, the networks' and stations' only product offered for sale is empty air—portions of blank air time in little packets of ten to sixty seconds, which are sold to advertisers for as much as a million dollars apiece. Empty air at those prices results in television, including the networks and the 800-odd commercial stations, enjoying sales of more than eight billion dollars annually.

The beginning script writer may envision this torrential flood of money cascading through the television industry and think that surely he or she should be able to dip into it for a cupful without too much trouble. Unfortunately, there's a catch. The very fact that there *is* so much money in television results in a mechanism which might be called the inspiration of fear.

The people who are supposed to make decisions in network television (and, to varying degrees, in local TV as well) are the ones who have cups—and even buckets—dipped into the river of money flowing through the industry. They get a lot of money, through salaries, expenses and other income sources, and many of them are terrified of losing it. They do not want to be accused of making a mistake, and so each decision is a risk. The result is that they often try to make a "fail safe" decision. For example, say a programming executive must decide between two programs. One, fresh and novel in its approach, is very well conceived and written. The other, a clumsily camouflaged clone of a successful program already on the air, has a mediocre script. The programmer is no fool; he recognizes the merit of the first show versus the second. But the second one is the safe choice, because it is just like the hit show already running. While if he chose the first show and it failed, he would have no excuse whatever for his mistake.

In this same vein, some story editors, when examining offered scripts, look with more interest at the credits of the script writer than at the contents of the script. If their choice is between a brilliant script by an unknown versus a ground-out formula script by some hack who has written for a dozen series, the hack is the safer choice.

The prime defense the new script writer has against the deep caution which motivates so many people in television is a script (or story outline) which is so impeccably professional-looking that it allays—or at least does not overly provoke—the recipient's instinctive reluctance to make an "unsafe" decision. In one important way, this all can work to the advantage of new script writers, for once they break through and make the first sale, the rest get easier each time.

If the movie industry went through a major change, the television industry is changing literally before our eyes. Forces are at work which are altering the structure of television as it has been operating since its inception. What people see on their TV screens no longer is exclusively the output of the three networks and the local stations, for broadcasting is now challenged by those engaged in "narrowcasting." There are so-called superstations which beam their lineup of programs via satellite to other local stations across the country, and there will be more. More producers of programs are bypassing the networks to set up their own distribution of their shows directly to the stations which buy them. Video cassettes and video disks are making it possible for a home viewer to watch an entire evening of programming on a TV set without ever tuning in to a local station. And cable systems, able to split their output into dozens of subchannels catering to many specialized tastes, are satisfying a need which could never be satisfied by the networks' mass-market approach to programming.

These developments—and others on the horizon—augur a new day in television, in which viewers will enjoy a bonanza of choices in their viewing. More important for movie and television writers, both veteran and new, this proliferation of program sources means an ever-increasing opening of new markets for scripts. For no matter how complex and sophisticated the technology becomes, from earth stations to laser beam transmission, it will always depend on what the poet Rimbaud called the "alchemy of the word."

# 2
# Writing for the Visual Media

The basic principles of writing stories were formed and developed long ago, when what we call a writer was really a talker. The advent of writing did not change the basic principles, since it only added the asset of permanency to the story-telling. The introduction of the first visual medium, stage plays, brought with it the first significant change in the craft of story-telling. There was now the enormous novelty of bringing the story to life; the audience no longer was "told about" John and Mary's problems with their love life—they actually *saw* John and Mary *having* their problems.

But while the authors of plays enjoyed the advantage of this tremendous impact on the audience, they paid for it by having to work within the limits of the new medium. The scope of action was confined to the finite dimensions of the stage, and the transitions were limited by how fast scenery could be changed and actors could get out of one costume and into another. (It is significant that while the person who creates a story for the printed page is called a *writer,* the person creating a play is called a *wright,* which seems to denote that a playwright, like a cartwright, is someone who fashions a tangible product which works.)

The next major visual medium, the moving pictures, had all the visual impact of a play but without any of the restrictions of the stage. A character did not have to step before a painted backdrop of the Golden Gate and say, "Well, here we are in San Francisco." The audience could see him get on a train or a plane and soon *be* in San Francisco, with the real Golden Gate Bridge behind him. But this advantage, too, had its price. Now, along with the aesthetic considerations the artist had to deal with, came clanking the new factor of Technology—cameras, sound recording, lighting, film editing, optical effects, film labs and more. With the advent of television came still another and different technology.

While the creative act of writing a story remains basically the same for the print and visual media, there are important differences in the *application* of the basics; and within the visual media there are differences in the techniques of writing for the screen and writing for television, arising out of the two different technologies. Obviously, the most effective script will be written by the writer who is familiar with these technologies—who knows the potential (and the limitations) of film and television production. But for the moment we are concerned with what comes before production: *writing* for the visual media. And the first priority of the script writer is the ability to think in visual terms.

Writers vary in their capacity to think visually. Some writers feel more comfortable using their creative talents in the nonvisual media; they feel the need to communicate directly with their audience (the reader) in verbal explanations and interpretations. They want to *tell* their audience what is happening and why, not show them. Such writers probably never feel the desire to write a script (or to buy or read a book such as this).

Other writers may prefer one medium but can generally move from it to another, depending on how a particular story best lends itself to being created and presented (or, more often, what can best be sold at any given time).

An example of this kind of writer is John Steinbeck, who is primarily known—in fact renowned—as the author of books. Although many of his printed stories have been made into movies, when one thinks of "the works of John Steinbeck" a bookshelf comes to mind, rather than a movie or television screen. Yet, when he felt it appropriate, Steinbeck could creatively think and write directly for the visual media. Significantly, when his novels, including such masterworks as *The Grapes of Wrath* and *Of Mice and Men,* were adapted for the screen he usually left the script writing to others. When he did write screenplays, they generally were original stories created especially for production as movies. And it is evident that Steinbeck remained Steinbeck no matter what medium he used, for his screenwriting earned three Academy Award nominations: Best Original Story of 1944 for *Lifeboat;* Best Original Story of 1945 (with co-writer Jack Wagner) for *A Medal for Benny;* and Best Story and Screenplay of 1952 for *Viva Zapata!* (which remains a legendary motion picture).

Reflecting on Steinbeck's three Academy Award nominations, I wonder how he would have fared if he had chosen to personally write the screenplays for the movie versions of all his great novels. In dealing with the stories and characters which first were born in his mind as creatures of the printed page, would the fires of his talent have burned as brightly in adapting them to this different medium? We will never know the answer—but I think he hints at it in his demonstrated inclination to leave his printed works as printed works and think originally when he turned to the screen.

Another kind of writer, somewhat in the minority, are the ones who feel the spur to *show it, not tell it* in what they write. Their characters act out much, or even most, of what these writers wish to convey. Only sparingly do they use the Omniscient Author's Voice and its frequent narrative monologues about what is happening and what it all means. These are the visual writers. When they write scripts for movies or television, the media suit their talents and creative processes. When they write for print, their work is usually characterized by a style that is more apt to be called "lively" than "wordy."

A prominent example of this kind of writer is Ernest Hemingway. Analysts of his style have emphasized that it is "spare," and a major reason for this quality is that his writing typically avoids frequent use of the long author-to-reader passages found in many other authors' work. Hemingway probably would have found it easy to write original scripts for films or television if he had wanted to, and the writers hired to adapt his work for the screen probably found the assignments easier than those involving other authors. It is not simply because Hemingway was a "great" author that so many of his novels have been turned into successful movies such as *A Farewell to Arms, For Whom the Bell Tolls,* and *To Have and Have Not* among others; there are other and even greater authors whose work has never really been captured successfully in a movie (despite Hollywood's appetite for story material cloaked in the aura of "certified greatness"). The reason lies closer to the fact that Hemingway was primarily a visual writer.

The 1946 movie *The Killers,* based on a Hemingway short story of that title, earned four Academy Award nominations. It is significant in Hollywood circles as the film in which Burt Lancaster made his movie debut. To me, however, it is significant for its opening nine and a half minutes, which has an impact out of all proportion to the rest of the movie. This opening sequence, despite its brevity, is a memorable example of movie drama.

Hemingway's short story concerns two professional hired killers who arrive in a small town one night and wait in a diner for their victim. He doesn't show up and they leave. One of the customers then goes to warn the victim, who thanks him but says he can do nothing but wait for it to happen.

Since not even Hollywood had the nerve to blow up a twelve-page episode in a diner into a 105-minute epic (no matter how lavish they made the diner or how many big stars they squeezed into the booths), the script writer, Anthony Veiller (who earned an Oscar nomination for his screenplay), simply took the story as written, made it the opening of the picture, and then went on with an invention of why the killers were after Burt Lancaster, using lengthy flashbacks.

The significant point is that Veiller incorporated the short story into his screenplay almost exactly as Hemingway wrote it. The nine and one-half-minute opening segment is a rare example of a story written for the printed page being transferred almost directly to film, with a minimum of tinkering to accommodate one medium to the other. Seldom can this be done with the work of most authors, and never with the work of authors who are not primarily visual writers. Because Hemingway *was* such a writer, it worked beautifully.*

When the creative juices flow, the script writer, as opposed to the prose writer, mentally sees his work *happening*—not *being read.* Let us observe the novelist or short story writer, sitting at his work table, doing what most writers do—"writing" in his head before he actually uses his typewriter or pen:

> *As Edward walked along the dark street he became aware of two things, both of which surprised him. First, the footsteps which were following him stayed behind too regularly to be a coincidence. Second, he not only was scared but he had been scared for the past half-hour, long before the footsteps had been noticed.*

As he sees it in his head the prose writer sets it down on paper. But the script writer with the same thought cannot merely formulate it into words and transfer those words to paper; he must think in terms of his medium, and that means he must think of it as it will appear on a screen. *His thinking— even before his writing—must be visual.* Instead of seeing words in his mind, he mentally sees

> *A shot of Edward walking briskly on a dark street. He becomes aware of something, slows down and listens.*
>
> *A close shot of somebody else's feet walking the same pavement behind him.*
>
> *Back to the previous shot of Edward as he continues to walk briskly. Noticing something about his hand, he raises it and is surprised to see it is trembling.*

What happened to the minor but interesting side fact that he discovers he not only is scared but *has* been scared for a

---

* A sidelight which illustrates television's role as primarily a sales (rather than a communications) medium: I recently noticed *The Killers* was scheduled as a late night movie on a local TV station. Staying up to enjoy it, I found that the station had made the movie fit that night's commercial lineup by simply eliminating the memorable opening sequence entirely and starting the movie right afterward.

half-hour without realizing it? It is out, because the effort (on the part of the writer, the director and the crew) required to convey it to the viewer would be far greater than the point is worth. Doesn't the script writer feel a slight twinge of regret at losing this literary equivalent of a grace note? No, because the experienced script writer doesn't think of such subtleties in the first place unless they can reasonably be conveyed on the screen. (Score one point for the creative advantage of writing for print over writing for the visual media—but before you post the final score, remember all the creative advantages offered by the impact of a story coming alive before the audiences' eyes. The look on the face of a wife fending off a husband's unwanted touch, especially in closeup, is worth a dozen subtle niceties possible only in print.)

Just as there is a difference in what goes on in the heads of a print author and a script writer as they sit poised to create, there is a difference in the mental processes of the writer of a theatrical motion picture and the writer for television.

Planning what he will write, the movie writer is relatively free to let his creative flow carry him wherever it may, within the confines only of the film technology and the general movie length the budget will allow. The budget is no mystery to the script writer. If he is working on assignment under a contract, he generally knows the precise figure. If there is some doubt about exactly how much money has been allotted or planned for production of the picture, he at least knows whether or not the cost is more than one million dollars because, under the Writers Guild contract, the minimum fee he gets for a so-called "flat deal" writing assignment is either for a "high budget" (more than a million dollars) or a "low budget" (less than a million dollars) production.

The budget will influence the movie writer not so much in creating the story as in the way it might be developed. The spectacular chase across the Alps and the villain's fall from the Matterhorn in the high-budget script would be the exciting (if less spectacular) chase across the Los Angeles rooftops and the bad guy's fall from the eighteenth floor of an office building in the low-budget script. Thus, except for specific detail, the movie writer's primary consideration is the age-old dramatist's concern for plot, characterization and motivation.

For the television writer, however, it is a different story—both figuratively *and* literally. The television writer must deliberately control his creativity to flow within the unnatural confines of something which rigidly prescribes exactly how his story must develop: *the commercial format,* which decrees that the story will be interrupted on the average of every eleven and one-half minutes.

If a writer knows in advance that his story will definitely be interrupted approximately every eleven and one-half minutes he obviously should write a story which *can* be so interrupted, which will make sense with those interruptions. Here we have the basic difference between movie writing and television writing. A screen story and a television story are not only different in their form and development but in their very genesis in the writer's mind. For example, as a writer contemplates an hour-or-longer story for television, letting his mind range free to seek story ideas, he might avoid as an unnecessary challenge a drama based on the confrontation between two people in a one-room snowbound cabin. Such a story would require long scenes (due to the nature of the drama as well as the physical setting), and interruptions on the average of every eleven or twelve minutes would be unnatural, giving the story a choppy effect. (It is the variety of changing locales and the sequence of short scenes that mask the choppiness of the average television story.)

To clearly illustrate how the commercial format separates television writing from theatrical film writing, let us imagine a line on a graph. This line represents the dramatic development of a story. Each square represents approximately four minutes of elapsed time. Thus the line on the graph will give a picture of (a) how often a dramatic peak is reached and (b) how long these dramatic scenes last, or how long they take to build.

A typical portion of a theatrical movie might look something like this:

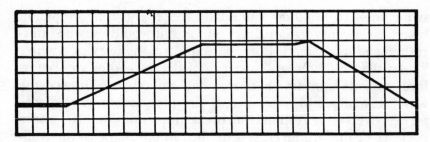

or this:

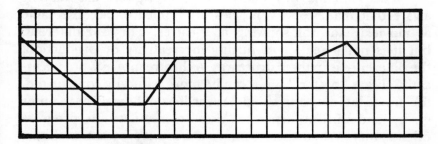

The possibilities, of course, are infinite, since each story's dramatic development will be different. Some gentle little tales will produce an almost straight line, while some potboilers will have a line that looks like the Rockies.

The same kind of graph representing the dramatic development of a movie made especially for television will, more often than not, look something like this:

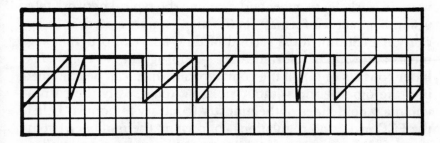

The reasons are simple. Usually in a TV-movie no scene can last more than sixteen to nineteen minutes. Thus, there is no point to building a dramatic scene whose development takes, say, twenty-two or thirty minutes; it would only be interrupted and its dramatic flow aborted. Also, the television writer knows that the interruptions are not fleeting—they can last as long as four minutes or more—and this must influence the way the writer ends each act. If the pressure to "hook" the viewer over each commercial break does not come from the network or the producer, it is implicit in the shape of the commercial format.

This explains why many television viewers are vaguely aware that made-for-TV movies are somehow not the same as movies made for showing in theatres. They *are* different, but it is not a matter of quality in creativity or production; the difference is in their structures. A theatre movie is not necessarily always "better," but it can be more naturally constructed, the drama building as it should, regardless of how many minutes go by, and with no separate "acts" to regulate the progress of the story. When theatre movies are put into the multi-act format of television the great scenes we recall from seeing the picture in a movie house often aren't as great as we remembered. While sometimes it is the effect of time on our memories, more often it is the effect of the TV editor's knife on the film. For this reason, many of today's movie directors insist on the contractual right to supervise the editing of their pictures into the necessary "acts" if the property later is sold to television.

Since it wields such an influence on the television script writer's work, let us meet and examine the typical network television commercial format. Its function, simply stated, is to apportion each individual second of time between program segments and what is referred to as "nonprogram material." The latter consists of (a) all the commercials which can be crammed into the time period without violating too grossly the current voluntary guidelines of the industry (contrary to popular belief, the FCC makes no regulations concerning the number of commercials in any program); (b) "promos," or promotional trailers for upcoming programs; and (c) public service announcements (Red Cross, United Fund, etc.), which ostensibly demonstrate the network's or local station's fulfillment of its responsibility to the community (but in reality often mean that one of the scheduled commercials was canceled at the last moment).

A program's commercial format on any of the three major networks, as shown on the following pages, will vary from day to day, depending on the number of commercials sold and the length of the particular show after being edited for broadcast. One interesting feature that remains the same is the pattern of the breaks for a movie. As shown, the early acts are long, to get the viewer "into" the movie. Then the commercial interruptions come more frequently, until the act in the very middle of the time period is a scant nine minutes of movie. Then the acts increase in length until, like the first, the last act is quite long, to soften the impression of the previous acts throughout the movie, which were only half as long as the opening and closing segments of the film.

The first brief glance, even more than a careful study of the following formats (especially the first, for two-hour movies), provides a vivid visual impression of what actually happens to a script when it appears in its natural environment.

```
 9:00:00   SPECIAL MOVIE TEASER OPENING — :60
 9:01:00   MOVIE: ACT ONE — 19:34
 9:20:34   COMMERCIALS (4 × :30) — 2:00
 9:22:34   MOVIE: ACT TWO — 11:53
 9:34:27   COMMERCIALS (4 × :30) — 2:00
 9:36:27   SHOW BUMPER — :07
 9:36:34   NETWORK IDENTIFICATION (PROMO) — :21
 9:36:55   Local station break — :34
 9:37:29   SHOW BUMPER — :09
 9:37:38   MOVIE: ACT THREE — 10:43
 9:48:21   COMMERCIALS (4 × :30) + PROMO — 2:30
 9:50:51   MOVIE: ACT FOUR — 12:05
10:02:56   COMMERCIALS (4 × :30) — 2:00
10:04:56   SHOW BUMPER — :07
10:05:03   NETWORK IDENTIFICATION (PROMO) — :11
10:05:14   Local station break — 1:44
10:06:58   SHOW BUMPER — :09
10:07:07   MOVIE ACT FIVE — 9:43
10:16:50   COMMERCIALS (4 × :30) — 2:00
10:18:50   SHOW BUMPER — :07
10:18:57   NETWORK IDENTIFICATION (PROMO) — :21
10:19:18   Local station break — 1:04
10:20:22   SHOW BUMPER — :09
10:20:31   MOVIE ACT SIX — 13:16
10:33:47   COMMERCIALS (4 × :30) — 2:00
10:35:47   MOVIE: ACT SEVEN — 19:43
10:55:30   COMMERCIALS (4 × :30) — 2:00
10:57:30   GOOD NIGHT (v/o) — :12
10:57:42   MOVIE CREDITS (+ v/o promo) — 1:03
10:58:45   MOVIE SERIES TITLE SLIDE — :05
10:58:50   NETWORK IDENTIFICATION (PROMO) — :06
10:58:56   Local station break — 1:04
```

```
                    Act 1 — 19:34
                    Act 2 — 11:53
                    Act 3 — 10:43
                    Act 4 — 12:05
                    Act 5 —  9:43
                    Act 6 — 13:16
                    Act 7 — 19:43
Total movie time        1:36:57  (1 hr., 36 min.,
                                      57 sec.)


(Total non-movie material, 23:03)
```

**Typical Network TV Format: Two-hour Movie at 9:00 PM**

18

```
8:00:00    SPECIAL NETWORK OPENING—:05
8:00:05    PROGRAM OPENING—:56
8:01:01    COMMERCIALS (2 × :30)—:60
8:02:01    PROGRAM: ACT ONE—16:01
8:18:02    COMMERCIALS (3 × :30)—1:30
8:19:32    NETWORK PROMO—:10
8:19:42    PROGRAM: ACT TWO—9:41
8:29:23    COMMERCIALS (2 × :30)—:60
8:30:23    PROGRAM TITLE—:10
8:30:33    NETWORK IDENTIFICATION (PROMO)—:21
8:30:54    Local station break—1:04
8:31:58    PROGRAM: ACT THREE—10:27
8:42:25    COMMERCIALS(3×:30)+NETWORK PROMOS—1:50
8:44:15    PROGRAM: ACT FOUR—11:19
8:55:34    COMMERCIALS (2 × :30)—:60
8:56:34    PROGRAM TRAILER (re next week)—:31
8:57:05    PROGRAM CREDITS—:30
8:57:35    NETWORK NEWS INSERT—:60
8:58:35    NETWORK IDENTIFICATION (PROMO)—:21
8:58:56    Local station break—1:04

                   Program opening      :56
                   Act One            16:01
                   Act Two             9:41
                   Act Three          10:27
                   Act Four           11:19
                   Total program      48:24
```

**Typical Network TV Format: One Hour Drama at 8:00 PM**

```
8:00:00   PROGRAM OPENING TITLE—:05
8:00:05   PROGRAM OPENING (TEASER)—:51
8:00:56   COMMERCIALS (2 × :30)—:60
8:01:56   PROGRAM: ACT ONE—13:01
8:14:57   COMMERCIALS (2 × :30)—:60
8:15:57   PROGRAM: ACT TWO—9:58
8:25:55   COMMERCIALS (2 × :30)—:60
8:26:55   PROGRAM TAG & CREDITS (+ v/o promo)—:30
8:27:25   NETWORK PROMO—:10
8:27:35   PUBLIC SERVICE ANNOUNCEMENT—:60
8:28:35   NETWORK IDENTIFICATION (PROMO)—:21
8:28:56   Local station break—1:04

                          :51 teaser
                        13:01 Act One
                         9:58 Act Two
            total time: 23:50
```

**Typical Network TV Format: Half-hour Series Comedy at 8:00 PM**

*We have discussed some of the creative and technological aspects of writing for the visual media as opposed to writing for print, but I leave for last what might be called a philosophical consideration.*

*The prose writer has a simpler and much more direct contact with his audience than does the script writer. It is satisfying to know that, except for incursions of editors and the quirks of typesetting, one's thoughts (through one's words) are transmitted to one's audience with an intimacy which transcends time or space. As I sat an hour ago reading a book by Somerset Maugham, it truly was as if the author were whispering into my brain.*

*As a script writer, however, you will find interposed between you and your audience the two barrier-like conduits which the craft requires: the technology, and the small army of men and women who, each in their own way, will not only convey but also interpret your work.*

*There's no way around it: you must accept the fact that once you have written, your work is no longer truly "yours"; it belongs,*

20

*creatively, just as much to all the others who contribute their talent and skill to making it come alive. All the script writer can do to ease the post partum pangs is hope that his or her meaning is so clear that, while it may be susceptible to interpretation, it is not vulnerable to distortion.*

# 3
# The Professional
# Script Format

Before we approach the creative aspects of writing a script—plot, characterization, dialogue, camera directions and all the rest—you should meet and understand the professional script format, for you can better consider creative techniques after you have first mastered the vehicle for your creativity.

The work of the beginning script writer not only must be good, it must look absolutely professional. Except for having an uncle as a producer or story editor, this is really the only way your script can hope to penetrate the barriers it will often encounter until you have some all-important credits to your name. Thus, no matter how brilliant your work may be, it must appear in a form that inspires confidence.

This is consistent with one of the basic concepts in much of the communications field: Image Is Everything. The typical new company starting out in a communications-based business, whether it be a production house, a public relations firm or an agency, will often lavish as much of its budget as possible on gorgeous furniture and sleek appointments in its reception area and offices. The workrooms may be raggedly equipped, the staff sparse and the working capital tiny—but the potted plants and rich carpeting which greet the prospective customer inspire confidence, and that's the name of the game. The beginning writer plays it by making his or her script look completely professional from first glance to page-by-page examination.

The standard format for television and feature film scripts

is not hard to learn, *but it is important that you not only learn the rules but also understand the reasons behind them.*

Writers are basically artists, and there is something in every artist that cries out for freedom in expressing his or her talent. Some artists feel unable to function to their fullest potential when confined to set formats and requirements, and so they may create new vehicles for their artistic output, or even try to exercise their talent without any thought of a prearranged format. But unlike dancers, painters, novelists and others, script writers (and composers) are in a special category; they may certainly break with tradition and push into new frontiers in the *substance* of their work, but in creating and presenting it, they must use the standard formats of their fields—*because while they may control the creation of their material, the execution of it falls to others.* Thus a script format, like sheet music, is only partly an artist's canvas. It is also a set of plans or blueprints to be used by many others.

Theatre movies, of course, are produced on film, as are almost all made-for-TV movies (which often find their way to projectors in movie theatres here and abroad). With rare exceptions, all scripted one-hour programs on the networks are produced on film. About two-thirds of all network half-hour shows (which are mostly comedies) are produced via videotape, as are almost all soap operas. Live television drama is just about extinct, but it may, like other endangered species, still be glimpsed on rare occasions. The format of a script for videotape or live television will be discussed separately. First let us turn to the senior medium.

## SCRIPTING FOR FILM

It is important to note that there is very little difference in physical format between the script for a typical teleplay and the script for a feature film produced for movie theatres. After a promising but brief flowering as a new and different medium, television, alas, mostly settled into becoming another part of the Hollywood entertainment factory. The majority of scripted television shows are produced on film, using the same technology and the same technicians associated with the conventional movie industry. Thus, except for length and separation into segments (or acts) to accommodate commercial breaks, most television scripts are almost identical in appearance to movie screenplays.

On the following pages you will find three consecutive pages of a typical film script. Read them and study them. Then I'll meet you on page 30 and we will go back and build them together, step by step.

INT. LIVING ROOM OF McCONNELL HOUSE - EVENING

A typical upper middle class suburban home. BILL, a fortyish
stockbroker, sits on the couch, looking over some papers
from his attache case. LAURA, his wife, enters.

                    LAURA
          Dinner will be ready soon.

                    BILL
          Good. I'm starved, but I want
          to finish this report first.
          I hate to have this stuff
          haunting me while I'm trying
          to have a quiet dinner.

                    LAURA
          Well, according to my timer,
          the roast will be ready in
          eleven minutes.

                    BILL
          The devil with your timer!
          It'll take me as long as it
          takes me.

                    LAURA
          I only meant --

                    BILL
               (apologetic)
          I know what you meant.

                    LAURA
          You're tired. I understand.

                    BILL
          It's more than that.
               (fishing cigarette
                out of pocket)
          This project is getting to me.

He gets up, goes to the fireplace mantel, takes the lighter
sitting there and lights his cigarette.

                    BILL (CONT.)
          There are more than two hundred
          separate reports to work up.

                    LAURA
          You can handle it. Especially
          with Irwin to help you. You're
               (MORE)

CONTINUED

CONTINUED

> LAURA (CONT.)
> lucky you have somebody working
> with you on it.

> BILL
> Well, at least I got home to
> dinner. Irwin got stuck or
> something on his half of the
> report. I offered to stay and
> help him, but he insisted that
> he could handle it. Practically
> pushed me out the door. He's
> still at the office now.

> LAURA
> Poor Irwin.

INT. IRWIN'S OFFICE - NIGHT

IRWIN, slightly older than Bill, works at his desk under a
small desk lamp. His phone RINGS. He answers it.

> IRWIN
> Gorman. Oh, hello, Mr. Bradley.
> Yes, I'm still here, plugging
> away. Bill? No, sir. He left a
> couple of hours ago, maybe more.
> Where? Well, he said he was going
> home, to have dinner. No, sir, I
> don't mind. I know how important
> this account is. Thank you, sir.
> Good night.

He hangs up the phone and returns for a moment to the work
he left. Pursing his lips thoughtfully, he poises his pencil
over it.

CU - PORTION OF HIS DESK

revealing a partly finished crossword puzzle.

WIDER SHOT

as Irwin uses his pencil to fill in one word. Then he puts
the newspaper containing the crossword into his attache case,
gets his hat and coat from a nearby rack, puts out the lamp
and leaves.

EXT. SUBURBAN RAILROAD STATION PLATFORM - MORNING

The commuters are waiting for a train, some reading their
newspapers, others chatting, a few sipping coffee from paper cups.

TWO-SHOT - BILL AND IRWIN ON THE PLATFORM

                         BILL
               When did you finally get out
               of there last night?

                         IRWIN
                    (scanning his
                    newspaper)
               A half hour or so after you
               did. As I was leaving, old
               man Bradley called.

                         BILL
               I had a feeling he might.
                    (being casual by
                    lighting cigarette)
               Uh, what did you tell him?

                         IRWIN
               Don't worry. I covered for you.

CLOSE - BILL

as he puffs his cigarette and gives Irwin a long, thoughtful look.

                              DISSOLVE TO:

INT. MR. BRADLEY'S OFFICE - DAY

A lavish, impressive high executive's office. MR. BRADLEY,
about fifty, expensively dressed and groomed, is on the phone.
His tone indicates that he is talking to someone with longer and
sharper fangs than he has in their corporate jungle.

                         BRADLEY
               Good morning, sir. The Great
               Eastern project? It's going
               well. We'll make our deadline.
               Yes, sir. I'm right on top of
               it, personally.

He hangs up the phone and turns to use the intercom on his desk.

                         BRADLEY (CONT.)
               Larry, I want you to quietly get
               somebody ready to step in and take
               over for one of the men on the
               Great Eastern account. No, no --
               just as a precaution. And make
               sure he's not a clock watcher,
               someone who'll give it his all.
               Someone like Irwin.

Looking at the sample pages even briefly, you will notice two basic characteristics of any professional film script.

**(1) All descriptions and directions are typed across the page, from margin to margin if necessary. All dialogue, and cues for how dialogue should be spoken, are typed in a narrow column, approximately three inches wide, in the center of the page.**

This physically separates the directions/descriptions from the dialogue, and like other aspects of the professional script format is simply based on clarity. In this case clarity is doubly needed: first when the script is being perused, so that the sense of what is said and an image of what is happening both flow smoothly and clearly in any reader's mind; and later when the script is being used, so that like any good workplan it may be translated into action easily and effectively (and, it is hoped, as the writer envisioned).

**(2) Double-spacing is always used to separate one element from another.**

It separates the basic scene identification line from the stage directions below it, the stage directions from the actors' dialogue, the dialogue of one actor from the dialogue of another actor, etc. (In the individual bits of dialogue the character's name, the speech and how it should be said are all considered as one element, and thus not separated by double-spacing.) But double-spacing is *only* used in creating white space to separate the elements on a script page. *All the dialogue, stage directions, camera directions, scene descriptions—in fact, everything in the script—is single-spaced.*

The first scene of any production typically fades in from a blank screen (either black or white), and thus the phrase **FADE IN:** is the screen playwright's traditional way of announcing the rise of the opening curtain on the work. It appears flush left.

If the script is of a teleplay, which the writer has divided into the appropriate number of acts,* then before the phrase

---

* In Public Television there is no commercial format and therefore no need for act divisions. However, it might be wise to somehow indicate where breaks could best be made in any teleplay longer than one hour, since ninety-minute and two-hour programs may be interrupted by on-air fund drives.

**FADE IN:** at the top of this page (and all subsequent pages where new acts begin) the designation of the act is centered, in capitals, and usually underlined:

<u>ACT ONE</u>

FADE IN:

One of the key components of the script is the line which identifies each new scene, typed all in capital letters, and always conveying the same three basic items of information: whether the scene is interior (INT.) or exterior (EXT.), where the scene is set, and what time of day it is supposed to be.

INT. LIVING ROOM OF McCONNELL HOUSE - EVENING

This goes to the heart of the script's use as a set of plans, even at the most preliminary stages. People concerned with budgets can go over a script to check all the INT.'s and EXT.'s to determine how many scenes will be shot inside a studio and how many will require more costly location shooting. They may also scan the scene descriptions (even before the set designer does so) to gauge how many separate sets will have to be constructed, and how simple or elaborate they will be. The director may check the number of different scenes and where they are set to gain a general impression of the scope of the production. Later, when the script is in production, the set designers, camera personnel, lighting director and others get their basic working cues from this line for every scene that is to be shot. This is an important line to know and to use properly, for it appears more often than any other element in a script, imparting key information to many people concerned with the production.

Below the line which identifies the scene we see a paragraph containing a brief description of the setting, the characters present in the scene and what they are doing:

INT. LIVING ROOM OF McCONNELL HOUSE – EVENING

A typical upper middle class suburban home. BILL, a fortyish stockbroker, sits on the couch, looking over some papers from his attache case. LAURA, his wife, enters.

The description of the set is terse, detailed only enough to convey what the writer thinks is important to tell about the McConnells' home. (William Shakespeare was a pretty good script writer and his stage setting directions were notably succinct, seldom going beyond a few words such as *An Apartment in the Castle.*) There should be no more detail than absolutely necessary because the writer's function here is to provide an *impression* of the McConnell living room as he or she envisions it, not to describe it down to the last item of furniture. That would impinge on the responsibilities (not to mention the ego) of the art director.

In certain specific situations the script writer may very well be justified in providing some descriptive details which are important to plot or characterization. For example, a woman is visiting the home of a man for the first time. They recently met and she knows he was previously married. But not until he lets her into his home does she realize that he has children: the familiar signs of wear on furniture, the toys visible here and there, all silently give her the news. Having her learn the fact this way, before he tells her, is a nice little dramatic device, and it satisfies the visual writer's dictum, *show it, don't say it.* Except for occasional situations like this one, a terse yet communicative description such as our "typical upper middle class suburban home" is sufficient.

In most cases the significant aspect of a scene is who we see in it. In this one we meet BILL and his wife LAURA. *The first time any character appears in the script the name or designation is fully capitalized.* Even if the character appears briefly one time only, capitals are used for that one time.

Every character of any importance should be introduced with some kind of description, but in no more detail than is necessary for purposes of plot or characterization. In the vast majority of cases, putting him or her in an age bracket is all that is needed, as in describing Bill as "fortyish." Referring to him as a stockbroker imparts, in one word, an adequate general impression of how he is dressed.

"LAURA, his wife" conveys, to the professional eye, all the essential data. The name is capitalized because it is her first appearance in the script. Her age is obviously a few years younger than Bill's by clear implication, since if it were a factor in the story (for example, a man married to a woman much younger or older than is thought usual) it would be specified. Her description simply as a [stockbroker's] wife is guidance enough for her general physical appearance and perhaps even her manner. Since these three words suffice for this character in this story, why use any more? In a script's descriptions and directions, conciseness is a mark of the professional; gratuitous rambling (even though only a few words) is not.

The use of a general age bracket is a familiar practice in professional scripts, and for a good reason. Except for special cases, descriptions such as "Joe, a short, stocky man with red hair" would place an unnecessary restriction on the casting director—if the instructions were followed, which is doubtful. (No casting director would bypass dozens of good actors who would otherwise be excellent in the role, just because they were of medium height or had black hair.) There will, of course, be times when your story requires a character to be portrayed as tall or blonde or lame, and on those occasions the requirement will be met, either by appropriate casting, by makeup skills, or a combination of both. I am aware that in the flush of creativity the good writer vividly envisions each major character in lifelike detail; but that usually should remain the writer's own private view.

The scene has been set, the characters introduced, and now comes the lifeblood of the script: the dialogue. Consistent with its importance, the script format provides for the dialogue's clear separation from all the rest of the material on the page. The character's name (usually capitalized in the dialogue por-

‌

tions throughout the script) is centered on the page, and his or her spoken lines are centered directly below:

LAURA
Dinner will be ready soon.

After a few exchanges of dialogue, we see that the writer considers it necessary to indicate how a line should be spoken, by typing the cue in parentheses just below and a few spaces to the left of the character's name:

BILL
(apologetic)
I know what you meant.

As with details of scenery and character descriptions, the script writer should be sparing with instructions about how an actor should deliver a line or perform an action. (The reader, I hope, has by now perceived a pattern concerning how far the professional script writer goes in telling his unseen colleagues how to do their various jobs.) A good rule for dialogue cues can be stated quite clearly: *Never indicate how a line should be spoken unless there is a definite possibility that without your guidance the actor will say the line improperly.*

Consider our sample scene. A few lines earlier, there is no advice from the script writer about Bill's response to Laura's comment that the timer shows the roast will be ready in eleven minutes:

BILL
The devil with your timer!
It'll take me as long as it
takes me.

Even without the exclamation mark, the sudden asperity with which these words are said is obvious in the words themselves. But Bill's next line, "I know what you meant.", is an ideal example of when instructions from the script writer *are* necessary. See how it would look without the cue:

```
                    BILL
          The devil with your timer!
          It'll take me as long as it
          takes me.

                    LAURA
          I only meant --

                    BILL
          I know what you meant.
```

With no information as to the writer's intention, the actor would be justified in assuming that Bill, still irritated, would say this line as sharply as the previous ones. But here the writer envisions the previous outburst as only a momentary lapse, a brief insight into the tension Bill is feeling. He is supposed to instantly regret his harsh reaction, and thus to show it by saying "I know what you meant." softly, reassuringly, more or less as an implicit apology for blowing up at his innocent wife. Since in this particular case the words themselves do *not* clearly indicate how they really should be spoken, the writer must step in to guide the actor.

Superfluous coaching of the actors is common to the scripts of most beginning writers (and even a number of veterans). Apparently they feel the need to typographically be on the set, coaching the actor in the appropriate emotion to display. It is a practice the script writer should avoid for a number of sound reasons which go beyond the chance of irking a few actors.

For one, it can be decidedly counterproductive. I have had some experience with actors and actresses, working with them as a writer, directing them (even going so far as to marry one). When they look over a script and see that the dialogue is chock full of all those adverbs in parentheses ("sadly," "joyfully," "hesitantly," "hastily"), most of which they recognize as unnecessary, they see them as clutter, and tend to ignore them all. Since your motive is to make sure the line will be read properly, using instructions sparingly—only for lines that are definitely susceptible to misreading—makes it more likely that each one will have the effect you intend.

We now see that the writer has given the actor some stage directions concerning some action to be taken while he is speaking his lines:

```
               BILL
       It's more than that.
          (fishing cigarette
          out of pocket)
       This project is getting to me.
```

Having the instructions appear in this position—in the same place as instructions for how a line is to be said—indicates that this bit of business does not necessarily interrupt the flow of the dialogue. It may be a single action:

```
               JUDGE
          (banging gavel)
       I've heard enough! Sit down.
```

Or a series of actions during the dialogue:

```
               JUDGE
          (banging gavel)
       I've heard enough! Sit down.
       You're out of order, and
       almost in contempt. This
       brief --
          (waves brief in air)
       -- is all I need. If you
       persist in your argument, you
       face a fine.
```

                    (turns to witness)
          I want you to ignore what you
          just heard.


   Like stage directions, instructions for how a line should
be delivered may also appear a number of times in the same
bit of dialogue. Sometimes the two kinds of instructions appear
together in an actor's lines:


                       GENERAL
          The enemy knows what we're
          doing, and when.
                    (angrily)
          He's not guessing, he <u>knows</u>.
          You know what that means.
                    (quietly, menacing)
          And what will happen to each
          of you if it doesn't stop.
                    (goes to map)
          He hit us here, and here. But
          if he hits us <u>here</u>, tomorrow --
                    (looks around at staff)
          Well, he better <u>not</u>.
                    (suddenly gentle)
          Men. . .I don't have to tell
          you what your duty is.


   The general's little speech fairly bristles with directions.
The ones concerning his actions need no justification, but test
the three which tell him how to say his lines against the guideline
set forth in italics on page 34.
   To return to Bill McConnell, sitting on his couch, we now
see that the writer wants him to get up, go somewhere and
do something:


          This project is getting to me.


He gets up, goes to the fireplace mantel, takes the
lighter sitting there and lights his cigarette.

The fact that these directions appear where they do, rather than within his dialogue, indicates that the action interrupts his speech. (If the actor is given so much action to perform *while* speaking that the directions would be too lengthy to be written in parentheses within the dialogue column, they would appear in the same place as the fireplace mantel business above, preceded by some phrase such as "As he speaks, Bill. . .")

Each time an actor's dialogue resumes after it has been typographically interrupted for some reason, it is customary to add some abbreviation for CONTINUING after the name:

```
                BILL (CONT.)
     There are more than two hundred
```

Since our scene continues to the next page, the word CONTINUED is typed in capital letters in the lower right corner of the page and as the first item at the top of the next page. This procedure is followed for as long as any scene continues over succeeding pages. You will also notice that Laura did not complete her bit of dialogue at the bottom of the page, and this fact is duly noted in the appropriate place:

```
     with Irwin to help you. You're

                (MORE)
```

This business of CONTINUED, (CONT.) and (MORE) may, depending on your mood when reading it, appear to be somewhat more explicit than a seemingly simple subject warrants. But simple though these particular typist's rules may seem, they carry a disproportionate burden of importance, since they so closely affect the *continuity of comprehension* of anybody reading or working with the script. While this factor is important in any kind of manuscript, it is especially critical in the case of a television or movie script *because the people using it as their working instructions will usually do so while far away from the writer.*

Thus your script must be completely self-explanatory, and to this end the typing customs just discussed, like other parts of the format, have been evolved so that clarity goes out of its way to manifest itself.

Now we are out of the McConnell living room and in Irwin's office, where we see him working at his desk as his phone RINGS. (Capitalizing all sound effects is not a firm rule; many experienced script writers do it, but some do not.)

In Irwin's first line we see the abbreviation *Mr.*, which is one of the few permissible exceptions to the rule *No abbreviations or symbols in the dialogue.* It is an easy rule to forget in the flush of writing dialogue in a rushing tide from the writer's mind onto the page, especially with words that are more commonly abbreviated than spelled out, such as *inc.* and *dept.* and *$5.00.* It is important always to remember that, unlike all the rest of the script, the dialogue is not written for the eye to read but for the mouth to speak. Thus the only abbreviations used in script dialogue are of those few words which are actually *more* familiar in that form than spelled out, such as *Mr.*, *Mrs.* and *Dr.*, which would be instantly read as they should be spoken without any hesitation by the actor.

We come at last to the glamorous star of all the elements in a script, the camera shot. All the various shots and moves of the camera will be discussed fully in Chapter 7, but here and now we are concerned only with the writer as typist and what goes where on a script page.

**All camera directions are typed in capitals. Each new camera direction should be isolated from the rest of your directions/descriptions by double-spacing and placed at the left margin.**

An example is page 28's

CU - PORTION OF HIS DESK

revealing a partly finished crossword puzzle.

The same applies to the change to the wider angle which immediately follows, and to the two-shot and close shot on page 29.

Camera directions within a scene which do *not* represent a change to a new angle, but are merely a modification of an existing camera shot (widening or narrowing the view, for example), while still capitalized, may sometimes be seen within a paragraph of other directions. For example:

```
CLOSE SHOT - TOM

as he walks along a corridor, frowning. WIDEN to
reveal that it is the corridor of a hospital. He stops
at one door and hesitates.
```

Midway in page 29, we come to an indication of how the writer envisions the transition from one scene to another, in this case a dissolve. Like camera shots and moves, scene transitions will be covered fully in Chapter 7, but here we are primarily concerned with typing considerations. In this case they are simple enough. **When a type of scene transition is suggested, it is always capitalized and isolated between the two scenes by double-spacing.**

Scene transitions (CUT TO, DISSOLVE TO, FADES, etc.) are almost always found at or near the right margin, as on our sample script. (The exception is the previously mentioned FADE IN: which begins the script, or an act, traditionally appearing flush left on the page.) Putting scene transition suggestions near the right margin separates them from the camera directions at the left, since they relate not to camera work but to editing after shooting is over. Again, clarity.

We now have discussed some of the most frequently used elements of a script, all of which are illustrated on our three sample pages. These are the scripting workhorses used on almost every page of a screenplay. Let us now discuss how to handle other writing/typing situations which might arise at least once in any typical script.

*Unseen Sound and Action*   When dialogue is spoken by an actor who is not directly in the scene, the letters O.S. or O.C. appear after the name:

```
            ELIZABETH
        (calling into
         other room)
  Jack! Come get your dinner.


            JACK (O.S.)
  I'll be there in a minute.
```

O.C. stands for *off camera*, O.S. for *off screen*. Whichever pair of letters is used, they are usually capitalized when typed after a name in the dialogue, as above. When they are used in descriptions or directions, they may or may not be capitalized:

```
As his fellow surgeons watch intently around the
operating table, Hoffman selects a scalpel and, with a
determined thrust, he makes the o.s. incision in the
patient's chest.
```

Thus the viewer would see the surgeon's gesture, but the actual "incision" would be framed by the camera to be just out of viewing range.

Sometimes a voice is heard over a scene where there is no other dialogue, such as a character telling about a dream which we see enacted, or an announcer narrating a documentary sequence. This is known as voice-over-film, generally indicated by typing V/O after the character's name. The same method applies to a particular shot in a scene which is "captioned" by some dialogue, as in this example:

```
John takes the photo out of the detective's hand and
looks at it.

CU - THE PHOTO
```

                              JOHN (V/O)
                    This is my brother. I'm
                    sure of it.

WIDE SHOT

as John hands the photo back, sighing sadly.

*Simultaneous Dialogue*   Sometimes in a scene there is primary dialogue against a background of secondary dialogue coming from perhaps a movie or television screen, or from another conversation nearby, as in a restaurant or on a bus. Unless this secondary dialogue is intended to be mere babble, barely intelligible, some actor or actors will have to say specific words, and the script writer must provide them. Often the secondary dialogue is meaningful, and the writer intends the viewer to get the drift of it even while the primary dialogue is being heard. (The relative volume levels of the two will be adjusted later at a sound-mixing session.) In any case, both dialogues appear side-by-side on the script page.

   In the following example our two primary characters, Vince and Lila, are having a conversation in their living room, while on their television set a doctor is consulting with his woman patient in a soap opera.

|  |  |
|---|---|
| **VINCE**<br>Face it, we got troubles, baby. Real troubles. | **DOCTOR**<br>I'm sorry, Ethel. The tests don't look good. |
| **LILA**<br>We can face them, hon. As long as we got each other. | **PATIENT**<br>Is it cancer, doctor? |
| | **DOCTOR**<br>I wish it were only that. |
| **VINCE**<br>I don't know. The furnace is ready to blow. The roof is so patched up there's nowhere to put another shingle -- | **PATIENT**<br>Oh my! What. . .what else? |

**42**

                    LILA                              DOCTOR
We'll pull out of it.              Your heart. It doesn't
Somehow.                           look good, I'm afraid.
                                   The strain of your kidney
                    VINCE          failure has weakened the
Somehow! That ain't                heart muscle.
enough. The sky's fallin'
in on us and you give me                         PATIENT
"somehow!"                         I've had some heart pain,
                                   ever since the murder. Do
                    LILA           I need another operation?
We can't just quit. We've
got to face it. We've got                        DOCTOR
to have faith that we can          I'm afraid you do.
come out of this --
                                                 PATIENT
                    VINCE          I hope they'll have the
               (bitterly)          proper facilities in
Yeah -- "somehow."                 prison.

    *Telephone Conversations*   When the writer intends to cut
back and forth to show both parties during a telephone conversation, it is not necessary to laboriously set and reset the scene
each time the switch takes place. Instead, the notation INTER-
CUT PHONE CONVERSATION may be inserted at the point
where the intercutting is to begin.
    Of course, this convenient script-typing shortcut cannot
be implemented until the scenes and characters on both ends
of the telephone line have been properly introduced and described:


INT. SQUAD ROOM - NIGHT


Rosetti and Klein are going over ballistics reports.
The phone RINGS. Rosetti answers it.

                    ROSETTI
               Homicide. Rosetti.

INT. CORNER OF EMPTY TV STUDIO - NIGHT

                        **43**

```
Sonny Hansen, clipboard and stopwatch in one hand,
uses a wall phone.

                    HANSEN
          Sonny Hansen, Sergeant. I
          think I remembered that
          license number.

INTERCUT PHONE CONVERSATION

                    ROSETTI
          Great. What is it?

                    HANSEN
          Well, it's really only an
          impression. . .
```

Sometimes the writer is satisfied to show only one side of the conversation, but wants the audience to hear the telephonic voice of the other party. This may be done by scripting the conversation in usual dialogue form, with the unseen person's lines notated each time as follows:

```
                    HENSHAW'S VOICE (FILTER)
          Good evening. Jones
          residence. Henshaw speaking.
```

*Ringing Down the Curtain*   Two of the sweetest words in the script writer's lexicon are FADE OUT, when used to signal the final curtain (and the end of the writer's labors, heralding a reunion with family, friends and the outside world). If it is indeed the last page of the script in the typewriter, what usually follows is the phrase THE END, and the final lines of a typical script might look like this:

```
walking on the beach with a confident stride. She
waves to the far-off figure, now recognizable as
Michael, as he races happily to meet her.

                              FADE OUT.

              THE END
```

If what is fading out is not yet the last scene of the story, but only the last scene of one of the acts in a teleplay, the format remains the same but the words END OF ACT TWO are used. It is good form to end each act on its own page, always starting the next act at the top of the following page.

## SCRIPTING FOR VIDEOTAPE AND LIVE TELEVISION

The script format for a play to be shot by television cameras, feeding what they "see" directly to a transmitter or to a video-tape recorder, has its origins in the early days of television, when there was no tape and everything was live. In those days, the standard TV script page was neatly divided: video (all action and camera directions) on the left, audio (dialogue and sound cues) on the right.

Dissatisfaction eventually set in with the video/audio for-mat. For one thing, it was a writing-typing nightmare. Just as important, the video part of the page did not leave the director enough room to jot down his planned camera shots. The result was a series of variations, until most writers settled on one called the NBC standard format in which all audio and video is combined in one wider column occupying about two-thirds of the page, to the left. (It was basically a radio script with some camera directions stuck in.)

It also suited the directors, who now had a third of each page kept blank for them, to fill in with camera shots of their own and other directorial notations. The script format used today for videotape, and also for live television drama (when you can find it), is a direct descendant of this format, and it bears a family resemblance to its ancestor.

Compared to the film script format, today's videotape/live TV script format is much simpler. It contains fewer camera directions, and much of what is carefully separated in a film script is combined in a videotape/live script.

The most noticeable characteristics of a typical videotape/ live script are:

1. It is all confined to the left two-thirds of the page.
2. All of the writer's directions and descriptions are in capital letters and, except for camera directions, are in parentheses.
3. Everything, including dialogue, is double-spaced.
4. The writer's cues about how dialogue should be said, and what an actor should do while speaking, are flush left like all other directions.

These are the principal typographical differences between a videotape/live script and a film script. Apart from these, the two script formats are generally similar, as in the fact that dialogue in both formats is typed in upper- and lowercase letters and centered in the typing area.

The following is a sample of typical videotape/live scripting. For comparative purposes, it is this format's version of the sample film script page shown on page 27.

CUT TO:
(LIVING ROOM OF McCONNELLS' SUBURBAN
HOME. BILL, A FORTYISH STOCKBROKER,
SITS ON THE COUCH, LOOKING OVER PAPERS
FROM ATTACHE CASE. LAURA, HIS WIFE,
ENTERS.)

                    LAURA:
Dinner will be ready soon.
                    BILL:
Good. I'm starved, but I want to
finish this report first. I hate
to have this stuff haunting me
while I'm trying to have a quiet
dinner.
                    LAURA:
Well, according to my timer, the
roast will be ready in eleven
minutes.
                    BILL:
The devil with your timer! It'll
take me as long as it takes me.
                    LAURA:
I only meant --
                    BILL:
(APOLOGETIC)
I know what you meant.

            LAURA:
You're tired. I understand.
            BILL:
It's more than that.
(FISHING CIGARETTE OUT OF POCKET)
    This project is getting to me.
(BILL GOES TO FIREPLACE MANTEL, TAKES
THE LIGHTER SITTING THERE AND LIGHTS
HIS CIGARETTE)
            BILL (CONT.):
There are more than two hundred
separate reports to work up.
            LAURA:
You can handle it. Especially
with Irwin to help you. You're

As you see, the one page of film script took about a page and a half in videotape/live script form. It is evident that the two formats are identical in one important characteristic: the dialogue is unmistakably separated from everything else on the page—for no matter whether the production is filmed, taped or live, the script is meant to be *used*, and therefore clarity is a constant consideration.

It should be noted that the scripting procedures for videotape/live production are not as strictly standardized as those for film scripts. Many professional script writers use their own minor variations (including the use of some film script elements in a videotape script).

## PROFESSIONAL SCRIPT LENGTHS

Length is an important factor in the professional script format, especially in television, where the writer is dealing with specific time slots. Obviously, all professional scripts cannot have *exactly* the same number of pages each time, not only because each script has different scenes, requiring varying amounts of words to describe, but also because no two writers will use the same number of words in handling the same scene. The following Guide, therefore, does not purport to show precisely how many pages each kind of script "must" contain. The numbers are approximate, but they do reflect a realistic average. The Guide's primary purpose is to shepherd you into remaining somewhere in the safe area, your scripts not noticeably longer or shorter than they should be.

A first glance could give the impression that television scripts run about a-page-a-minute, but that is deceptive. While it is close (a rough average might be one and one-fifth pages for each minute), it must be remembered that commercial breaks reduce the amount of story time in a program's time slot. A "thirty-minute show," for example, will actually contain about twenty-three and a half minutes of scripted program, a

SCRIPT LENGTH GUIDE

| SCRIPT | PAGES: FILM | PAGES: TAPE | ACTS |
|---|---|---|---|
| Half-hour teleplay | 30 | 45 | Two |
| One-hour teleplay | 60 | 90 | Four |
| Ninety-minute teleplay | 90 | 135 | Six |
| Two-hour teleplay or made-for-TV movie | 113 110 | 170 165 | Six or Seven |
| One and one-half hour theatre movie | 105 | No act divisions and not usually videotaped. | |
| Two-hour theatre movie | 137 | | |

"sixty-minute show" may have forty-eight minutes and twenty-three seconds, etc. The Guide takes these factors into consideration and the numbers are adjusted to reflect scripted story time, not total program time.

While the number of acts shown for television scripts is more or less standard, their individual lengths will vary from one program series to another. Also, each series has its own format. For example, many programs have a "teaser" of approximately one minute which precedes Act One. (This holds the viewer during a subsequent break for some commercials before the show has even really started.) How to determine the particular format for any program for which you want to write, along with the question of how to know whether a program is produced on film or videotape, will be discussed in Chapter 8.

You need not be concerned with making each act of a television script the same length. Some acts can be a bit longer, some a bit shorter, depending on the way your story develops, as long as the total number of script pages is within the boundaries indicated by the numbers in the Guide. (Once your script is sold, the story editor may, if necessary, edit your script to fit precise needs.)

In the case of a screenplay for a theatrical feature there is, of course, no "time slot." Movies produced specifically for showing in theatres can be as short as an hour and twenty minutes, epics running four hours or more, or anywhere in between. But the reality is that few beginning screenwriters can sell a script for an epic movie (even if they write one). Movies are incredibly expensive to make, and more incredibly complicated to finance, and even the most receptive producer would wince at the prospect of trying to gather all those extra millions to gamble on the work of an unknown and untried screenwriter. Thus if you are reading this book, rather than some notes for your Academy Award acceptance speech, you would be well advised to keep your screenplays from going much beyond 150 pages. For that reason the outer boundary for theatrical features in the Guide is 137 pages, which is the mean average of the 125 to 150 pages found in the typical professional screenplay for a two-hour movie.

## TITLE PAGE AND CAST LIST

Since the first thing anyone will see in your script is the title page, simple as it may be it will convey that important first impression of you and your work. While there are variations in title page arrangement, there is a general "look" that all professional scripts have when you open the cover.

1. If it is a teleplay, the title of the program series for which the script was written appears as the first line.
2. Next below (but first if it is a theatre or TV movie), the title of the script, in quotation marks and underlined.
3. Next below that, the kind of authorship involved:
   If the work is original—*Written by* if it is a movie *or* teleplay, but *Original Screenplay by* only if it is a movie.

If the script is based on another source—*Screenplay by* if a movie; *Teleplay by* if for a television program.

4. The name(s) of the script writer(s) next, also on a separate line.
5. If the script is based on another source,* next comes the attribution, such as *Based on a story by Alex Jackinson.*
6. In the lower left or lower right corner, indicate whether it is a First Draft, Second Draft, etc., or Final Draft, and the date either when the script was completed or when it was submitted.
7. In the opposite lower corner: the name, address and telephone number of the script writer or, if there is one, the writer's agent.

Except for the last two items, which should appear in the corners, it is optional whether you center the information on the page, type it flush right, or whatever—as long as it appears on separate lines and in the order shown above. The choice of all capitals or not is also optional for any particular line (although it is more customary for the writer's name to appear in upper- and lowercase letters).

The page following the title page should be the Cast List, containing all the characters in your script. Any character important enough to have been described in the script should be tersely described after his or her name on this list. Usually the age will be sufficient. (Of course, if the character is a regular in a television series no description is necessary.)

Next, although it is not absolutely necessary (nor always expected), a page listing all the sets involved, separated as to whether interior or exterior, might help toward creating a good first impression.

*As mentioned earlier, we have discussed the basic, most frequently used script elements, plus others which can be expected to come up regularly in script writing. But there are others, which will probably never come up in one of your scripts—but could conceivably come up in any of them.*

---

* The need for obtaining written permission before submitting your script based on someone else's material is discussed in Chapter 8.

*What will guide you to do the "right" thing, I hope, will be your realization that the script format is not some ritual formula, but a sensible tool developed for clarity of communication between the script writer and those who will later use the script. Your idea may be unusual, even unprecedented, but as long as you express it clearly, and in a way that is consistent with What Goes Where on a script page, it will look professional, and much more important, will be understood.*

# 4
# Creating Stories
# and Characters

Creating stories and the characters in them is what script writing is really all about. The rest—the technology, the business, the timing and the luck—are also found in a thousand other activities of life. But when, in the matrix of a blank page, a story starts to emerge which never before existed, and characters are born and develop who never lived before that moment, something very special is happening. It is part craft, part art and (there's no other word) part magic.

The magic of the creative process remains basically mysterious, like any other kind of birth. The art is a product of the artist's personality and thus differs with each person. But the craft is based on experience, common sense and professional techniques, and *can* be learned and practiced.

Principles and rules and fashions of playcraft change but one bedrock truth remains constant: *the basis of effective drama is conflict.* Learn this and you learn a lot. Sophocles knew it. Shakespeare knew it. And the writer of the script for that popular TV series you saw last Tuesday knew it. The conflict of man against man, man against woman, man against nature, man against himself—the clang of two opposing forces coming against each other makes for drama. The conflict may be Big and Important—the numberless masses tearing down the mighty regime of the Czar in *Dr. Zhivago.* Or it may be small and wistful—a fat, homely butcher and a plain neighborhood girl making a clumsy grab at a chance for love in *Marty.*

Consider one of the most successful motion pictures of

all time, *Gone With the Wind*. Along with her skill for recreating a colorful time and place and sheer story-telling art, Margaret Mitchell built her story with such effective dramatic conflicts that both the book and the movie are still very much alive (and making money) today. While the Civil War itself was not directly one of the conflicts (for conflict implies two opposing forces and the North almost never appears in her work), it served as a suitable backdrop for the interplays of strong dramatic conflicts with which the author fashioned her story and characters:

> The Old South versus the emerging reality of a new and different world.
>
> Rhett Butler, who could have any woman he wanted—*except* the one he wanted most:
>
> Scarlett O'Hara, beautiful enough to attract any man *she* wanted—except the one she wanted the most:
>
> Ashley Wilkes, torn between wanting Scarlett and needing Melanie.

These characters, with their frustrations and longings, could have become no more than soap opera figures—just as *Macbeth* could have become no more than a murder melodrama. The difference, in both cases, was that the authors had the gift of imparting life to their characters and meaning to their conflicts. Thus audiences *cared;* they still do.

Examine any good story and you will discover the conflict which motivates the main character(s) and moves the plot along. One of Somerset Maugham's most enduring stories is *Of Human Bondage*, whose very title highlights the conflict of the young surgeon fighting against his imprisoning love for a worthless girl. But just as enduring, if not as deep, are Laura Lee Hope's children's books about the Bobbsey Twins, each of which gets the kids into some conflict which, happily, is resolved in the final pages.

Sometimes if you look carefully you find the same basic

conflict in widely different stories. In *Tom Sawyer*, it is wanting to be good to a loved one (Aunt Polly) versus the pull of adventure with wilder companions. The same conflict (in a dog instead of a boy) is the basis for the drama in *The Call of the Wild.* And, in essence, nearly the same conflict is at the heart of the story of the opera *Carmen.*

The knowledge that conflict makes for drama is a nuts-and-bolts tool which writers can use—especially when they sit at their writing desk caught up in a conflict of their own, namely, "I've got a rough idea of a plot but I don't know what to do with it." First, *think of the plot in terms of the conflict or conflicts involved.* If you cannot identify any, you probably do not have the basis for a very strong story idea. This in itself is an accomplishment, for it can save hours of work, reams of paper and pangs of disappointment later.

What contributes drama to the plot is not the conflict itself, but rather what the character does and how he or she does it in response to that conflict. People are naturally more interested in people than they are in circumstances. What engages their attention is not so much the adventure as the adventurer, not the danger so much as how the people react to what is menacing them, not the surprise ending but how the characters in the story are affected by, and respond to, the surprise.

This simple but fundamental fact that people are primarily interested in people is the basis for another important tool of scriptcraft: *characterization,* the development in a character of specific personality traits. Examine most successful movies and television series and you will find they often have one thing in common: a well-drawn central character (or characters) whose personality traits are clearly defined. These traits may be good ones or bad ones but they are distinctive. Early in a movie, over the weeks in a TV series, these characteristics become familiar to the viewer. They add a dimension of depth and reality to the character. Another (and perhaps paramount) reason for the enduring success of *Gone With the Wind* is the author's skillful use of characterization; Rhett Butler and Scarlett O'Hara were so vividly conceived and depicted that millions of readers and viewers have found it impossible to believe they are not real people.

On television, the mortality rate of new programs is appalling. Not many new shows survive a season's journey through the ratings mine field. Half-hour comedies are especially popular with viewers, and so smoke pours out the stacks of the Hollywood fun factories day and night as they churn out an endless assembly line of new shows, in which "wacky" characters do "wacky" things— and get "wacky" ratings and disappear. Sometimes, before they expire, they are desperately switched from one time slot to another, scrambling around the network's program schedule like escaped hamsters.

Why do so few of them take root and prosper? The answer, I think, is that they are sitcoms, or situation comedies—which means their emphasis is on ever-zanier "situations," with the people in them seldom developed beyond the cartoon character stage. But there *are* half-hour comedies which become popular successes with longtime runs and high ratings. While they also may be called sitcoms in the trade, these shows might be more accurately called "charcoms," for their humor comes not from artificially contrived "situations," but from artfully created characterization.

Among them was one of the most successful television series of all time, *The Mary Tyler Moore Show,* which could have gone on forever, and ended only because the star probably grew tired of the weekly series grind. It immediately became one of the most successful products on the rerun circuit (establishing something of a record for the price paid for syndication rights). The secret of the show's success clearly was the effective characterization established by the original creators and skillfully followed by all the subsequent script writers. The funny situations almost always resulted from, or were related to, the regular cast's character traits, which were familiar to every viewer. Proof of the power of good characterization is the fact that no less than three of the show's characters were spun off into successful series of their own: *Rhoda, Phyllis* and *Lou Grant.*

What makes this kind of "charcom" so successful is also

what makes many dramatic series attain great popularity while their competition regularly arrives and departs. This includes action-adventure shows. *Kojak,* for example, was a tremendous hit, and still is, in its syndication afterlife. But *Kojak* was never really about cops-and-robbers and drug busts; it was primarily about Lieutenant Theo Kojak.

Therefore, whether you are writing a script for a television series, a single original teleplay or a movie, a prime factor to consider is the importance of character creation. Even when you feel your plot is the paramount consideration in a particular script, your characters should never be mere puppets manipulated to suit it. It does not always take a full-scale portrait to make a character come alive; sometimes a few well-drawn strokes can do it.

The best and strongest plots, however, are those which do evolve naturally, even inevitably, out of the characterization. These stories have more impact, because they are more believable. There is good reason for this. In the lives of most of us, very few important things happen for totally external reasons; what happens to us is often the result of what we do— and what we do is often the result of what we are. That is true of you and me and your potential viewers. If it is also true of your characters in what you make happen to them, they will be perceived not as concoctions, but as living characters with a dimension of depth and reality. Thus your story will not merely gain the attention of the audience, it will make some impact upon them. There's a difference; it means they will *care* about what they are watching. And, as producers, directors and story editors well know, when an audience feels an involvement, it shows in the ratings and at the box office.

Let us see an example of plot developing out of characterization. Jane is a timid young woman, terrified of asserting herself, due in large part to her overbearing mother. She is constantly driven to gain her mother's approval, seldom succeeding. A situation arises at work wherein problems are causing the company's management to consider going out of business. Jane, who has a keen and analytic mind, has diagnosed the problems and feels she has a solution that may save the company. The frantic meetings of the managers behind closed doors are getting louder each day.

Conflict: Jane's desire to offer her solution, thus possibly becoming a heroine, getting her reward and making her mother proud of her—versus her inability to push herself into the councils of upper management and possibly be rebuffed and humiliated. It's not *Hamlet,* but it is the basis for an interesting human drama with which an audience can identify.

The point is that the characterization I created for Jane does not function merely as a kind of outer garment she wears as she makes her way through the plot; the plot evolves directly out of her characterization. If I changed the kind of person Jane is, my plot would no longer work. The two—characterization and plot—are welded together.

Some writers may have an intuitive ability to create a fully defined character as they go along; however, it cannot hurt (and will always help) to first write a detailed sketch or profile of any major character. Creatively, the more you "know" about a character the more you contribute to his or her reality in the script. Practically, facets of the character's personality will often strongly suggest plot ideas. (When one of my characters is especially well defined, I occasionally become aware that he or she is really writing the scene, while I follow along at the typewriter, interested and even curious to find out what will happen next.)

However, writers do vary in both their skill and their inclination for characterization. For some writers, formulating a plot is paramount, and the people caught up in the action are merely vehicles to advance the story line. Obviously, if a plot is compelling enough, viewers will be interested in what is happening even though they are not particularly interested in those to whom it happens. Many movies and television series attest to this. While I believe a more memorable story will evolve out of characterization, I would much rather see a script with an intriguing plot moving at a well-orchestrated pace even though with cardboard characters, than one with vividly sketched characters whose personalities are fascinating, but *nothing really happens.*

There is a test the script writer should apply to his or her work as it proceeds to be sure that there is a consistent plausibility to the characters and the plot. The test is *motivation.* Motivation makes the difference between actions seeming real or staged. People are not robots; they generally do what they do for a reason. Sensible people act from sensible reasons and fools act from foolish reasons. The writer looks at each action of the main characters and asks, "Would this particular person do this, in this particular circumstance?"

The movies of the thirties and forties, mostly ground out by writers on a weekly salary, were often written as fast as they were typed, and frequently had no time to bother with motivation. Now they live on mainly at 2:30 A.M. on television and there is a reliable way to identify them in the TV listings: the word *decides.* "An heiress decides to run off with her gardener . . ." "A millionaire decides to take a slum kid into his household . . ." Whenever you see the word *decides* in a movie listing, you know that the only motivation involved is that it was Thursday and the script was due in the producer's office by Friday. When you look over your script after a cooling-off period, try to be objective enough to note whether your character "decides" to do something just because, solely for plot purposes, you want him to. If he does, if proper motivation is lacking, it is a sign that the scene (or possibly a larger segment of the script) requires rethinking and rewriting.

There is another element in any kind of story, one not so susceptible to definite guidelines. I refer to *theme.* Writers generally are writers because they have an inclination (or perhaps an impulsion) to communicate. But the reason any individual writes any particular story must vary, not only with each writer but with each story he or she writes. We all have different interests, different outlooks on life and different matters we consider important; if these motivate us when we sit down to do our communicating—our writing—our work will reflect a theme.

In a story, plot is what happens. Theme is the larger framework of meaning in which it happens. Larger stories have larger themes, and lesser stories have lesser themes. In the powerfully written and expansively produced *The Godfather,* the theme was that evil is self-consuming. In a program I saw last night in a half-hour comedy series, the theme was the importance of good friends later in life.

Do not confuse a theme with a "message." The writer should not be trying to make a commentary on his or her theme, only to *air* it. Reflection on the meaning should rest with the viewer.

Do all writers have themes for their stories? The answer is, not all the time (and not always consciously). But a theme is an asset to any literary work. First, it elevates the story because there is some central meaning to it all. Then, it assures a better, more unified construction to the script, for it provides a general reference point to guide the direction of the plot and the development of the characters.

Herman Melville wrote, "To produce a mighty book, you must choose a mighty theme." You will find, however, that when it happens, it is more as though the mighty theme chose *you.*

# 5
# The Script
# Outline

A writer heavy with script is like a woman heavy with child. After carrying the creation inside long enough, there comes a time for the delivery. When the plots and characters and bits of dialogue have percolated sufficiently in the mind, the writer feels the urge to find a piece of paper, and an outline is born.

The primal version of an outline is a *synopsis,* a short, terse indication of the basic storyline and its main characters. Since a synopsis conveys only the basic essentials of a screen story, it is possible for the synopsis of a four-hour movie to occupy only one or two typewritten pages. The brevity of a synopsis can serve a useful purpose, for in reducing the narrative to its barest form it can reveal the basic merit, or the basic flaws, of the prospective screen story.

An outline has two basic functions, one in the writer's workroom, the other outside it:

1. It is a tool the writer uses in developing a screen story to the point where it becomes a potential script, and then it is used in writing that script.

2. Out in the marketplace, a polished outline may be offered as a kind of "salesman" for the potential, unwritten script, and, if approved, lead to an assignment to write it. (Sometimes an outline is purchased as a story property, with someone else assigned to write the actual script.)

In the general conversational sense, an "outline" may be little more than a rough story idea scrawled on the back of an envelope, or it may be so complete and detailed that you could practically take it on the set and shoot the scenes from it. Or anything in between. But what is usually meant by an outline in professional movie and television circles is *a scene-by-scene description of the story, in narrative form.* It is, in fact, often called a *scene breakdown,* or simply a *breakdown.* And while it is not yet a script, it is script*oid,* and therefore all in the present tense: "They go out the door and he tells her that he loves her," etc. Outlines are double-spaced, and if for a teleplay or TV-movie, they are divided into the appropriate number of acts.

To illustrate what an outline might look like, and also how it relates to the script which will evolve from it, let us return once more to the saga of Bill McConnell in our sample film script on pages 27, 28 and 29. What follows is that portion of the outline (close to the final one) which was the basis for the four fully-scripted scenes on those three pages.

It's evening in the living room of the McConnell house in Scarsdale, a fashionable suburb of New York City. It is a typical upper middle class home. Bill, a hard-working Wall Street stockbroker in his forties, uncharacteristically snaps at his wife, Laura, who recognizes it as a sign that he is under a strain. Bill confirms this, revealing that he feels swamped by the burdens of the special project he has been assigned. She tries to reassure him by reminding him that he has someone to help him with the workload: his fellow worker, Irwin. Bill remarks that, late as it is, Irwin is still working down at the office.

At the office, Irwin *is* at work—doing a job on Bill. He's obviously just hanging around to see if the boss will telephone. The boss, Mr. Bradley, does call, and Irwin makes sure he gets the message that while good old Irwin is plugging away, Bill waltzed out early to enjoy dinner with his wife.

Next morning at the railroad station, Bill learns from Irwin that the boss called. Trying to keep it casual, Bill asks what Irwin told him. He hears Irwin reassure him that he "covered" for him. Somehow this choice of words does not sit well with

Bill, and we see by the way he looks at Irwin that he is starting to wonder if his co-worker is as uncomplicated and helpful as he seems.

That same day, Mr. Bradley, in the corporate stratosphere of his lavish office, quietly arranges for a possible replacement for Bill on the crucial project. Someone more reliable, he says, like Irwin.

We said this outline was close to the final one. What brings it closer is the inclusion of more details. The most completely detailed outline of all, after which (and from which) comes the actual script, is often called a *treatment.*

This fine old term harks back to the early days of Hollywood movie manufacturing. (A similar term, *scenario,* has failed to survive as well in modern professional use.) It is believed to have originated in the hunt for suitable story material for the new medium of moving pictures, whereby a writer would be asked to write something showing how a book or story or play could be "given the movie treatment," that is, successfully translated into a screenplay. Today it is used both with and without its earlier meaning of transmuting print into film, depending on whether it is called a *treatment* or an *original treatment.*

The fact that a treatment is more complete than the outlines which may precede it does not only mean that it includes more details and descriptions. It is more a matter of construction. The outline is a vehicle for conveying a screen story (and in fact is often called a *story outline* or *plot outline*). The treatment is more of a rudimentary screenplay—it conveys a visualization not only of the story, but also *how* that story would be presented on the screen. Thus a treatment not only provides more detail about what happens in a scene, it will include some specific camera angles and shots when the writer feels they are necessary to precisely convey what he or she envisions.

The same is true of dialogue in a treatment. An outline is primarily concerned with conveying *a sense* of what the characters say, seldom going beyond paraphrasing potential dialogue. In a treatment, however, key scenes may include some specific dialogue. For example, the very last lines of an *outline* for *Gone With the Wind* might be something like this:

> As is her way, Scarlett declines to face what has happened. Wearily climbing the stairs, she tells herself she doesn't have to think about it now. Today things may look black, but there is always tomorrow. . .

THE END

The very last lines of a *treatment* for the movie might be something like this:

> Scarlett stands there, in the silence of the huge empty hall. Then, wearily, she turns and starts to climb the great stairway. As she ascends, she speaks self-assuringly.

SCARLETT
Tomorrow at Tara I can face it.
I'll get him back somehow. After
all, tomorrow is another day.

SLOWLY:
FADE OUT.

THE END

As may be seen, in the outline it is the author who tells us that "Scarlett declines to face what has happened" (Rhett having walked out on her a few moments ago). But in the treatment, Scarlett herself *shows* (by her dialogue) that she declines to face what has happened.

An outline is the blood relative of a script and it shows that kinship by strictly confining itself to what can be seen and heard on a screen. But it is completely unlike a script in one meaningful characteristic—it is a literary work, in that *it is meant to be read.* Therefore, within the functional requirements of an outline, its author tries to make it a well-written work of prose.

There is no precise number of pages which an outline "should" be. The length of "your" outline—the one only you will see, in which you work everything out—will of course depend on you. But as for the scene breakdown outlines prepared for others to see, there are approximate dimensions familiar to people in the industry, and these are shown in the Guide.

As with the script length guidelines in Chapter 3, these numbers are only general averages, and subject to even more leeway because of the nature of an outline's contents. (An outline in the form of a treatment will be longer than the figures shown, but how much longer will depend upon how detailed it is.) As before, the Guide takes into consideration the actual length of teleplays and TV-movies, not the "program lengths" which include the commercial breaks.

| OUTLINE | APPROX. PAGES |
|---|---|
| Half-hour teleplay | 12 |
| One-hour teleplay | 20 |
| Ninety-minute teleplay | 35 |
| Two-hour teleplay or made-for-TV movie | 50 |
| Ninety-minute theatre movie | 45 |
| Two-hour theatre movie | 65 |

SCRIPT OUTLINE LENGTH GUIDE

The outline warrants your best creative effort, for it is in the outline, not the screenplay, that your creativity can best be implemented. A flash of inspiration can certainly come while writing in the more prescribed format of the script, but how much easier it is to change, to amplify, to insert, in the more accessible form of the outline.

It is in your outline that you assure a sound construction to your work as a whole. Your characters are born and established here. Your plot develops here. The dramatic continuity, so vital in the script to come, has its origin here.

Only when you have made it as much a reflection of your total creative intent as possible do you turn to the next stage— the script. That, in fact, is what it has all led to, for an outline has no real life of its own; it exists only for its metamorphosis.

# 6
# Writing the Script: Dialogue and Scenecraft

Plot lines, characterization, motivation and all the rest are to your script what brain and heart are to the body: lifegiving, but unseen. All that the outside world perceives is what your characters say and what they do—the dialogue and the action.

To write dialogue well, it is important to understand what it really is, what it isn't, and why. *The primary function of dialogue is to convey information to the audience.* The information may relate to plot, to character revelation, to locale—anything from the simple fact of what day it is to the profundity of what a character believes his or her life is all about. In actuality, *dialogue is not spoken from one character to another, but from the author to the audience, via the character.*

None of the dialogue in a script should ever be mere "filler," padding out a scene between what the writer considers the good lines or the important exchanges. Ideally, every line of dialogue should have a purpose. In most good scripts they do, although it may not always be readily apparent. Consider the following:

> WALLY
> Good morning, dear.

> EDNA
> 'Morning, hon. Pass
> the rolls, please.

**74**

At first glance this prosaic exchange of dialogue might seem innocent of any purpose such as relaying information. Surely it is nothing more than a script writer "getting into" a scene. But study it again, asking yourself, *what information does it impart to the audience?*

The answer is simply that it establishes the apparent state of the relationship between Wally and Edna, in this case a peaceful and pleasant one. Not earth-shaking news, I agree, but something the audience should know, and it has been unobtrusively told to them in the first five seconds of the scene. (If the two people had been shown sitting down to breakfast with curt, icy greetings followed by snarls back and forth, what the script writer was doing would be more obvious.)

There is a practical reason for not including any lines of dialogue which do not serve some useful purpose. In television the precious seconds are too fleeting, and in movie production they are too expensive, to be wasted. But there is another reason which is far more important: it will result in a higher quality of writing, which will be evident later on the screen. When every line of dialogue means something, or does something— when it is all meat and no fat—the script has an unmistakable vitality. It *moves,* with an irresistible pace that grasps the audience and draws it along from line to line and scene to scene. In the words of the industry, it "plays."

This is often accomplished not in the writing but in the cutting. The gold is there, but it cannot shine because it is obscured by the slag mixed in with it. John Steinbeck knew how important it is to remove this slag. In discussing his screenplay for *Viva Zapata!* with Elia Kazan, who was to direct it, he wrote: "I want to go over the dialogue once more for very small changes . . . in other words all filler wants to come out. There isn't much but there is some. *I'll want no word in dialogue that has not some definite reference to the story.'*

Recognizing and cutting out the fat in dialogue can be the hardest part of the job for many writers. This is especially

* Elaine Steinbeck and Robert Wallsten, eds., *Steinbeck: A Life in Letters* (New York: The Viking Press, 1975), p. 407. Italics added.

true when it comes to something that is undeniably well written but not strictly necessary. The courage to ruthlessly remove something clever from your work can come from asking yourself, *Is my ability to come up with good ideas so limited that I'd better use every one I get before the supply runs out?* If you have confidence in your creative powers you will dispassionately delete the line or the scene you are "in love" with, for the sake of improving the overall script. (If your confidence is less than total, you'll set it aside in hopes of perhaps using it elsewhere.) In any event, with experience should come the confidence that *you can spare any gem, because where it came from will come a thousand others just as good or even better.* If and when you truly believe that, you're a professional. And your writing will show it.

While the information being relayed to the audience by way of dialogue is often subtle, sometimes it is as plain as a character telling his wife, "I didn't get the promotion today." This is known to playwrights as *exposition,* whereby dialogue directly sets forth or explains facts.

*Excessive reliance on expository dialogue is one of the surest signs of a poorly written script.* When a screenplay or a teleplay appears "talky," the writer has neglected the unique qualities of the film and television media. A stage play may contain a greater proportion of expository dialogue because of the physical limitations imposed on the script by the theatre and the stage. But when writing a television or movie script, you can have your character seated at the table for Thanksgiving dinner with the family, and the next moment have him jump forward in time to the automobile drive home afterward. Or, for that matter, just as instantly backward in time to something that happened long before Thanksgiving which he now has reason to remember. Just as important, in a film or television script you have the incomparable advantage of the closeup, in which the raising of an eyebrow or the tightening of lips can have deep dramatic meaning, impossible for the stage character who can be sixty feet or more from the audience.

Therefore, since the screen, unlike the stage, never *forces* the writer to use expository dialogue, the film/television writer may (and should) use it only when it is convenient and appropriate.

While *show it, don't say it* is good advice for any film and television writer, like any good advice it must be used intelligently, for of course if everything is "shown" and nothing is "told," one may end up with a script requiring a thousand separate scenes. How, then, can you determine if and when you are misusing exposition, by putting into your characters' mouths what really should be fully enacted before the audience's eyes?

There are two kinds of general information conveyed in a script: facts about *events* which happen or have happened; and revelations about *people*, such as what they are like, how they act and react and what they feel.

Let us first examine events, such as the earlier example of a character telling his wife "I didn't get the promotion today." If the potential promotion has been established as a key event in the structure of the story, obviously you will write a scene wherein the promotion is denied. Or, if the promotion has received no particular mention, but part of the characterization you are developing concerns the employee's feelings about rejection, you may decide to put your character into a scene wherein the matter of promotion is raised but he learns he is passed over in favor of somebody else.

Equally clear could be the decision to script no special scene, but simply have your character say to his wife, "I didn't get the promotion today." This might be because your story concerns his wife's insatiable ambition and greed, which she tries to satisfy by pushing her husband beyond his capacities and inclination. Here, more important than seeing him lose the promotion would be seeing what happens when she hears about it from him.

So far we have dealt with scenes which clearly should, or just as clearly need not, be depicted. But now let us make a slight change in what happened down at the office, from "I didn't get the promotion today" to "I turned down the promotion today." Everything that applied in the three examples still holds true, but with an interesting added factor if our story concerns the third example, the insatiably ambitious wife pushing her reluctant husband.

One could still say that the news could be delivered in a line of dialogue, because seeing her reaction is more important than seeing what she is reacting to. But now, in deciding what to "show" and what to "tell," the writer might be influenced not only by what structurally *should* be shown, but also by what the writer feels the audience would *want* to be shown. In this example, turning down a promotion—saying no to more money, a bigger office, more authority and prestige—is not something the average person hears about every day. It is rare and somewhat fascinating. Thus, whether strictly necessary or not, it could be a mistake to risk disappointing the audience (even if only in some back alley of their consciousness) by making it a factor in the story and not showing them how it happened.

With experience, it usually becomes easy to decide that a certain event warrants a separate scene, and that another need only be mentioned in a line of dialogue. But whether a scene that isn't really necessary nevertheless is one that an audience would want to see, is not always a clear and immediate decision. Unlike the others, it is not a matter of technical criteria, for this kind of personal judgment does not relate to craft, but to art. It has been stressed that no line or scene should be included that does not serve a purpose. But that purpose need not be confined to matters of plot, characterization and motivation. Giving the audience a scene you feel they want to see is the very essence of good theatre—and *theatre*, more than anything else, is what the writing and production of movies and television shows is all about.

The other kind of information conveyed in a scene concerns not events but feelings, and here the writer is dealing with a vital element which can determine the quality of the script. The reason for this has already been touched on, in discussing the importance of characterization and its relationship to the story: people are primarily interested in people, more than events. A good script is one which gets the audience interested—but a great script is one that gets them *involved.* And what goes on *inside* your characters, more than what goes on in the story around them, is the key to gaining the involvement of the audience. Let us examine how and why that works, and more important, how you can get it to work for you as you write your script.

Involvement is largely a matter of identification. Let us say that you read two headlines on the front page of your newspaper: DEATHS REACH 200 IN SALWEEN RIVER FLOOD IN TIBET, and TWO CRITICALLY INJURED IN ROOF COLLAPSE AT LOCAL LIBRARY. Which story would you turn to first? If you are like most people, you probably would immediately want details of the library story. Objectively, you realize that two hundred deaths are more tragic than two injuries; but, subjectively, you can *identify* with the victims of your library's roof collapse.

So it is with an audience. For example, they watch a story about a businessman on a buying trip abroad, who finds himself caught up in the deadly intrigues of an international spy ring when he falls helplessly in love with a beautiful and ruthless adventuress. His life is in danger, his business is threatened and his illicit liaison may destroy his relationship with his wife and children.

In watching this movie or teleplay the dramatic action may hold their attention, but it is the emotions involved in the story which cause a personal response. After all, very few typical people ever have any contact with a spy ring. How many businessmen get the chance to be manipulated by a beautiful adventuress, or even meet one? How often in every day living does the average person find his or her life in danger?

But *fear* is all too familiar to all of us. The compulsions of love and sexual desire are part of almost everyone's experience. The tie that binds one to spouse and to children is a deeply meaningful part of real life. Common feelings, universal emotions—it is these in a script which can evoke a sense of *identification* in the viewer.

In writing the scenes wherein your characters' emotions

are revealed, it is especially important to know when using dialogue for exposition would be a mistake. Here, perhaps more than in any other area of the script, the principle of *show it, don't say it* pertains. If conveying your characters' emotions is important to your script, you want to do this with maximum impact. *What we see and conclude for ourselves has more impact than what we are merely told about.*

If, in your script, you want to convey to the audience a key fact, in this case that John loves Mary, you have three choices. First, you can put them in a suitably romantic setting and have John say some variant of the basic statement, "Mary, I love you." If your audience has been given no reason to doubt that John is a person of average sincerity, you have conveyed your information—in the convenient but adequate way it has been (and still is) done in countless scripts.

Second, stepping up from a scene that is merely adequate, you can put them in a situation which clearly is *not* suitably romantic—such as juggling packages on an escalator, or dodging cars as they cross in the middle of a busy street—and thus have it make more of an impression when John suddenly takes Mary's arm and says, with feeling, "I love you."

Or, best of all, you can see to it that the audience does *not* learn how John feels about Mary by hearing the words "I love you" come out of his mouth. Instead, John *demonstrates* his love in unmistakable ways. It can be through some major sacrifice he makes which could result in her happiness, or through a single meaningful gesture, such as his hand lingering tenderly on her face after what ostensibly was but an amiable pat on the cheek.

It need not be something he does. He can show how he feels by way of dialogue and still be demonstrating, rather than telling, his love. However it is done, if John's love for Mary is demonstrated, rather than only stated, something interesting happens: you have the audience working for you. They know he loves her, they accept that he loves her—because it is their own conclusion, formed in their own minds, based upon what they saw and interpreted for themselves.

This device for making the audience work for you in accepting some fact you want to convey has long been known and used by skillful propagandists and by writers of polemics. The best dramatic writers and directors employ the same device (although often quite intuitively) in their most memorable work.

Of course none of this means that your characters should never (or even seldom) verbalize what they are feeling. In the right scene, at the right time, nothing might be more natural, or useful in advancing the story, than for the person to say "I love you" or "I'm scared" or "I hate him." But when the emotion is particularly meaningful, this verbalization should only confirm what the audience already has seen or will see for themselves.

## THE ART OF WRITING DIALOGUE

So far we have discussed effective use of dialogue, but its most artful planning and application is irrelevant if the dialogue is not written so that it *sounds* right. *The art is in writing dialogue that sounds like people talking, not like a writer writing.*

When dialogue doesn't sound right, its artificiality is evident to the most casual observer. Surely you have watched a movie, a television drama or a stage play, and as the actors emitted interesting thoughts but in unconvincing and unnatural-sounding "conversation," you were clearly reminded of the clatter of the author's typewriter in every sentence. Good dialogue, on the other hand, is like fine cabinetry—the observer appreciates it without ever being made aware of the hand of the artisan in the work.

A familiar expression is that a writer who produces good dialogue "has a good ear." This is interpreted by many to mean that the writer has some unique talent for listening to others' conversations, and using this acuity to make script dialogue mirror everyday speech with particular accuracy. Those who think this are quite wrong. The talented script writer has "a good ear for dialogue" all right, but it is not where they think it is. It is not the ear outside the head, overhearing everyday conversations between people, but rather an inner ear that enables the writer to "hear" inside his or her own head the kind of dialogue that will sound right in a script. For it is a very special kind of "conversation" that is *not* as actual people talk in everyday life, *but gives the illusion that it is.*

The conversations that we all have in real life typically are full of half-finished sentences, circumlocutions, pauses, grunts and much repetition. If a writer were to faithfully reproduce this in the limited time frame of a scene, it would be accurate but eminently tedious. Besides, audiences expect that dialogue on the screen has some purpose beyond what they ordinarily hear in their own living rooms; after all, somebody went to the trouble of *writing* those words.

Dialogue, then, is what actual conversations *would be* like if many of the unnecessary words, speeches, sounds and pauses were edited out. However, the skillful writer's dialogue faithfully reflects the *patterns and rhythms* of real life conversation, and this is the key to whether or not the dialogue rings true.

Since different people have different patterns of speech, part of the secret of making your scripted characters come to life is to establish patterns of speech for them, and to make sure they consistently follow this pattern every time they speak. This also helps to give all your dialogue the illusion of realism, because two or more people talking together, each in his or her own particular way of speaking, is exactly what happens in real life; nothing could be more natural-sounding. When none of the characters consistently speak in a voice of their own, they all speak in the voice of the author, and this is why some dialogue sounds "written."

The difference between whether or not a key scene "plays" with memorable impact depends on another factor in dialogue writing: the author's awareness of the *rhythms* of speech, and how he or she uses them. Rhythm is vital to music, which is why so many combos, no matter how small, often include a bass player. The sounds that come out of the big fiddle may seem lost amid the loud volume of the trumpet and piano—but while the audience *hears* these other instruments, they *feel* the rhythm of the bass. It makes a difference. Similarly, while an audience hears the words in a powerful scene, they sense the rhythm of the dialogue (if the writer has put it there), and this is what makes the scene *move*.

Infusing dialogue with rhythm is partly a matter of bouncing one character's lines off another character's lines. As it builds, the last words of one are often a springboard for the first words of the other. This not only makes for a definable rhythm, it also creates a strong tide of continuity that sweeps the conversation along. When it is done right, the effect is there but it all seems so natural that "the hand of the artisan is never seen in the work."

A good example is the following, a key scene from the original screenplay by Gerald DiPego for "A Family Upside Down,"* a two hour dramatic special seen on the NBC Television Network in 1978. (I was with NBC at the time, and I recall that the quality of this production was like a balm to the wounds of that network, which was then at one of its sorriest low points in the long and bloody ratings war which reached a peak during the seventies.)

The story concerns a family wrenched by the heart attack of the elderly father, and this scene between the mother (Emma) and her married daughter (Wendy) takes place in the home of Wendy's brother, where the mother has been living.

INT. EMMA'S ROOM - NIGHT

She is sitting on the bed. Wendy is examining some of the things in the room, ambling about.

                    WENDY
          God,† I remember these books. You
          read me this Oz book chapter by . . .
                                        CONTINUED

* A Ross Hunter Production, Inc.
  Ross Hunter/Jacque Mapes
† Changed by NBC before air time to "Oh."

                    EMMA
            Wendy . . . I don't want to stay here
            any more.

Wendy stares, concerned.

                    EMMA
                 (continuing)
            Seeing Dad twice a week—it's just not
            enough. You're closer to the nursing
            home . . .

                    WENDY
            Mom, I . . .

                    EMMA
            If I stayed with you, maybe you could
            get me there every day, just for an hour
            or so every day . . .

                    WENDY
            Mom, I'll take you to see him tomorrow,
            and you're welcome to stay the
            weekend, but this is where . . .

                    EMMA
            Do you know what's happening to him?
            He's leaving us, Wendy. I have to *be*
            there. I have to keep him with us. Carol
            thinks twice a week is being with him.
            It's *not!* It's . . .

                    WENDY
            That's the best they can do! Mom,
            they've changed their lives. They've
            made a place for you in their lives. What
            do you want?!

                    EMMA
            I want to stay with you now.

                                    CONTINUED

> ### WENDY
> (knowing)
> No, you don't. You just want things to be the way they were. You and Dad together. Things can't be that way.

> ### EMMA
> Will you listen to me! He's dying!

> ### WENDY
> The Doctor said he . . .

> ### EMMA
> The Doctor knows nothing! *I* know. I know he needs me there to hold him. I'll hold him so he can't leave us. Wendy, please! I'm asking for one hour a day with him . . .

> ### WENDY
> An hour a day? What hour, Mom? I work every . . .

> ### EMMA
> After work.

> ### WENDY
> After work I'm tired. And my husband is tired . . .

> ### EMMA
> Wendy, I *need* you now!

> ### WENDY
> Al is going through a bad time. *He* needs me now. Can you understand . . .

CONTINUED

> EMMA
>
> Let *him* understand. Can't he understand that this is a crisis? It's a time of crisis.

> WENDY
>
> Yes! For me too, Mom. See, meanwhile *my* life is going on too. Do you want to hear about it?
> (near tears)
> I don't want my husband to leave me again. He left once. I never even told you. He came back and we're trying to work it out. You can't come and live with us now.
> (tears now)
> No. I'm saying no, Mom. I'm sorry. But my God, everybody's life is still going on. Mine and Mike's and Carol's. They have their problems and worries. Everybody's world can't revolve around visiting Dad. The Doctor said he's not in danger. He's not!

Wendy tries to fight the tears, stop crying. Emma is staring into space.

> EMMA
> (after a moment)
> You can leave me here tonight, then.

> WENDY
>
> Oh, Mom, come and stay the weekend.

> EMMA
>
> I don't want to.

> WENDY
> (exploding, tears
> again)

CONTINUED

CONTINUED

> I'm sorry things can't be the way you
> want them! I'm sorry I can't help. I'm
> sorry about everything, Mom.

DiPego's scene is intensely dramatic because capsulized in this one brief encounter are all the conflicts which form the dramatic basis for his plot. It provides an ideal example of lean dialogue: almost every line conveys something vital. And, during the heart of the scene, the rhythm is there, giving to the dialogue a momentum which, on the air, made the scene impossible to turn away from.

I like this brief scene because it demonstrates good script writing by a working professional plying his craft in the busy and often hectic atmosphere of the Hollywood creative environment, where the order so often is "I don't need it good, I need it Friday!" It is heartening to note that *both* these needs are regularly met by many writers and producers, proving that quality is possible to achieve despite the pressures of commercial television and movie production.

## DIALOGUE AND ACTION

Dialogue can no more be isolated from action in constructing a script than can melody and harmony in creating a symphony. The film or television writer makes it all actually happen in a twin flow of *they do . . . they say . . . they do . . . they do . . . they say . . .*

Dialogue and action work with, and for, each other in many different ways throughout a script. For example, the slamming of a door behind a character gives punctuation to what he or she says on the way out. Conversely, dialogue can be effective punctuation to action, as when a delivery man trips and almost falls over a roller skate in the driveway, and says, "Kids!"

Dialogue can provide a needed "breather" between sequences of intense action. But it should not just be filler when used for this purpose; the thoughtful writer saves something that should be conveyed in dialogue and then uses it on just such an occasion.

One interesting and effective way that dialogue is interwoven with action is as a kind of advance caption to a scene that follows. An illustration of this may be found in our sample film script in Chapter 3. At the end of the first scene and the beginning of the second we saw:

BILL
. . . He's still at the office now.

LAURA
Poor Irwin.

INT. IRWIN'S OFFICE - NIGHT

IRWIN, slightly older than Bill, works at his desk. . . . His phone RINGS. He answers it.

The final words in the dialogue of Bill and Laura were written specifically to serve a number of purposes. First, they make it possible to go directly to the key action of the next scene without the "establishing" which otherwise would be necessary to orient the viewer as to where the next scene is located and who is in it.* Further, it imparts to the scene transition a kind of "punch": *"He's at the office"*. . . *"Poor Irwin"*. . . *Bang— we see him.*

Then, from a creative standpoint, Laura's sincerely sympathetic "Poor Irwin" dramatically highlights the sly treachery which immediately follows. This technique of using the last words of a scene to caption the start of the next, when used properly, can heighten the drama that is in a scene, or provide an element of drama when it is lacking.

The action in a script is just as much a part of the "writing"

* The need for, and use of, establishing shots are discussed in the next chapter.

as the dialogue. Action can sometimes speak more eloquently than any words, for what a character does in a scene can be more revealing than what he or she says. This was notably demonstrated by *The Thief,* a 1952 spy melodrama starring Ray Milland, in which there was music and background sound but *not one word of dialogue.* The movie received excellent reviews.

Individual gestures can be effective because they are a universal language, instantly understood by the most diverse viewers. Spoken language is a sophisticated invention of civilization, but gestures go back to the cave. Thus they convey their meaning with a clarity and impact few words can achieve.

## DIALECTS AND ACCENTS

Dialogue which is to be spoken with a noticeable accent or in a dialect is an area of uncertainty for many beginning script writers, who often make the mistake of phonetically writing how they believe the words should be spoken. There are a number of things wrong with scripting something like the following (for a character who is supposed to speak in a thick southern accent):

> SHERIFF PURLY
> Waal, ah done rahtly know bout 'at 'ere.
> Y'all bout ta git yerseffs in a mahty big
> pecka trouble.

First of all, it would probably annoy the actor who plays the sheriff, for it implies that he is expected to laboriously study and memorize these eye-busting lines, mouthing the precise pronunciation provided. (Let the actor act.) Then, it would present the director with the unsolicited services of a remote control dialogue coach. (Let the director direct.) Finally, it presumes to set forth the exact pronunciation of the one particular accent which is accurate for that specific area; is the writer, in fact, an expert in regional phonemics? (Let the writer be a writer.)

The key to scripting dialogue for a character who speaks in a dialect or with an accent is to provide, not suggested pronunciation, but the *style and rhythm* that come from the appropriate words in the appropriate sentence form.

Our Sheriff Purly is an example of this, for even in plain spelling—

> Well, I don't rightly know about that
> there. You-all about to get yourselves
> in a mighty big peck of trouble.

—the lines unmistakably reflect the cadence and flavor of the dialect.

Similarly, what characterizes a foreign accent is not only the odd way the words are pronounced, but also the arrangement of the words in the sentence, which often reflects the syntax of the native language. For example, let us say a story concerns an old man who speaks with a marked Yiddish accent. He feels his family has wronged him in many ways, and now he resents that they are trying to get him to retire. In speaking to an old friend, he complains that they are now taking away his work.

Some writers might simply have him mispronounce some words in the familiar way and assume that they have him speaking with an accent: "Now they vant to take my vork away from me."

But what makes him "have an accent" is not only things like interchanging w's and v's, but that he often speaks English words in Yiddish sentences. If we script the line that way, even without the mispronunciation it will sound more accurate and realistic: "They want to take away from me my work, now."

Your characters should be described as speaking with a particular accent or dialect during their introduction in the script, or in their first bit of dialogue. Then, if you provide the appropriate words in the appropriate style, the actor will do the rest.

## TRANSIENT AND LOCALIZED SLANG

Nothing stamps a movie or teleplay as being dated so much as hearing "in" phrases that have since gone "out." Your story's basic appeal may be timeless, but one scene's passé dialogue can impart a faint air of mustiness to the whole production.

Theatre movies potentially have a very long life plus a possible afterlife on television, and teleplays can be veritably immortal via reruns. Knowing this, many producers do not like to see anything in a script that could interfere with an old bit of box office philosophy about a show always seeming fresh and brand-new to any audience that hasn't seen it.

More important to the script writer, unassigned free-lance scripts are not always bought by the first producer who sees them (or sometimes even the twelfth). The last thing a writer wants is for a potential buyer to know (or even to think) that the script now being considered has been shopped around, unsold, for months or even years. The colorful phrase so popular when you wrote the scene may be nostalgic memorabilia by the time the script is in the mails.

Good slang is pungent and pithy and it can make your dialogue sparkle. But there is a difference between slang that becomes accepted as a part of the language, and fads of speech that suddenly attain widespread currency and then just as suddenly drop out of favor and disappear from use. The wise script writer tests each word or phrase of slang about to be used in the script by trying to remember (or doing some research to determine) whether or not the expression has been around for awhile. If it has been in use for less than a year, avoid it, since the jury is still out and the verdict could go either way.

Even worse than expressions which the audience finds outdated are those which they find incomprehensible. Some "in" phrases are pervasively popular, but only in limited areas. (Although television broke forever the cultural isolation of the country's various regions, many fad phrases remain localized.) If you live in a large metropolitan area, you may hear a phrase being used "everywhere"—until you travel a hundred miles away. Before you put one of your longtime favorite turns of phrase into your script dialogue be sure that, unlike some Hollywood writers, you are not confusing *your* world with *the* world.

## TESTING AND TIMING YOUR DIALOGUE

Since dialogue is meant to be spoken, the only true test is not how it reads but how it sounds. And *you* should not be the one who reads it aloud to test it, for you will hear what you *want* it to sound like, and this may not be what it actually sounds like.

Before testing what you have written, put it away to marinate in the sauce of passing time for at least a day. (Good advice, I assure you, for *any* kind of writing.) Then, because the flush of creativity has cooled, you will examine it with a more objective eye. Whatever survives your deletions and changes may now be handed to someone who will read it aloud, while you listen and evaluate how realistic the dialogue sounds.

Timing the dialogue is important when writing a television script since, unlike a theatrical screenplay, it must fit a specific time slot. While you can only estimate the timing of the action in a scene, the dialogue can be timed to a closer approximation, helping to provide some idea of how each scene compares to the time schedule you have set for it.

A stopwatch is an extremely useful tool for any television writer (and they range from complex and costly to simple and inexpensive). Using the sweep second hand of a watch or clock is less accurate and less convenient than using a stopwatch, but if necessary it will prove adequate.

An important rule for timing dialogue is *never do it "in*

*your head.*" If you do, your timing will be inaccurate by at least 30 percent, and probably more. But let me show it, not say it. Try the following experiment. Take at least a half page of any reading matter and time how long it takes to read it silently. Then time yourself reading the same material aloud (and fully aloud, not mumbling under your breath).

The reason for the inevitable disparity is that, unlike when you read silently, it takes time to form each consonant with your lips and tongue, to manage your breath intake between commas and periods and to pronounce rather than merely "see" each word.

After you have timed the dialogue in a scene, it is a good idea to add about 25 percent more time, to account for variations in actors' readings, as well as for stage business and "body business" (chin rubbing, head scratching, etc.) during dialogue which you did not anticipate.

## THE SPECIAL NATURE OF SCREEN DIALOGUE

Our earlier chapter, *Writing for the Visual Media,* considered the differences in writing for print and writing for the movie and television screens. But one of the elemental differences was saved for mention here, as it concerns the very essence of dialogue.

It is interesting and somewhat ironic that, compared to its counterpart on the printed page, screen dialogue's greatest asset is at the same time a great drawback. Unlike printed dialogue, no one has to imagine what screen dialogue would sound like; they *hear* it. Thus while prose writers' words may approach realism, the words of the script writer achieve reality.

But it works both ways. For the very fact that screen dialogue *is* so lifelike means that it disappears upon being heard. Therefore, unlike printed dialogue, *it cannot be thoughtfully perused and studied.*

The transient nature of screen dialogue places on its writer a special burden. Besides trying to make it natural-sounding and meaningful, and sometimes dramatic, the script writer must also make sure that it is always completely comprehensible. Printed dialogue can be re-read, but screen dialogue cannot be re-heard. This means the script writer cannot use certain words or phrases which would be instantly recognizable in print but not when heard from the screen.

Not only the dialogue but the entire story on film or television *happens*. It moves along from word to word and scene to scene, like a train that rattles past the viewer's attention without stopping. Thus, *continuity of comprehension* on the part of the viewer is vital, and it can be impaired or destroyed by anything which interrupts it. A phrase some viewers did not quite understand, a statement profound enough to intrigue them but requiring them to analyze its import, a word that sounds enough like another word to momentarily confuse or mislead them—none of these belong in dialogue for the screen. But even more important than what you leave out, of course, is what you put in. Given the transient nature of screen dialogue, choose words and ideas which will instantly be understood.

*About 2,500 years ago, Themistocles wrote that "the speech of man is like embroidered tapestries." Let the tapestries you embroider be interesting and even subtle—as long as your design is clearly discerned.*

# 7
# The Writer and the Camera

*a mini course in
film/TV production*

Because the camera is the primary artistic tool of film and television production, many new script writers are fascinated by the opportunity to use and control it via their typewriters.

Directors, with justification, consider the camera "their" tool, and knowing this, those who advise beginning script writers usually suggest that they keep their camera directions to a minimum. (Including me, often in this book.) But it is a matter of avoiding excess in camera directions rather than shying away from them completely. For while it is true that the director's job is to choose precisely how each scene shall be shot, it is also true that when the red light goes on outside the studio door, the director can only shoot what the writer has provided.

The camera, then, may be in the hands of the director—but first it is in the mind of the writer.

This, in fact, is the very reason that scripts by experienced and talented writers usually do contain a minimum of specific camera shots and moves. These writers *think and write cinematically;* that is, in terms of what the camera shoots and how it shoots it. The requisite camera direction for much in their scenes is implicit in the composition and action of the scenes as written.

However, there are times when, to make his or her meaning known, the script writer must use the language of the camera. Thus you should learn it—but, as in learning any language, the more you know about the world from which it comes, the more intelligently and confidently you will use it. For that reason we will go beyond merely citing a list of camera terms, and try to make them more meaningfully understood from the deeper perspective of the working world in which they are used.

## SHOTS AND MOVES OF THE CAMERA

What a motion picture or television camera performs falls into two general categories: camera shots, which relate to the *purposes* of the filming; and camera moves, which relate to *ways* of accomplishing these shots. First let us examine camera shots.

*Establishing Shot*   The need for an establishing shot reflects one of the basic problems in presenting a story that moves across the screen. From opening credits to The End, as scenes change, and as angles within scenes change, there is a continual necessity to keep the viewer oriented as to *where we are now* and/or *what we are looking at.* To establish this, special shots, designed specifically for this purpose, start any scene which might at first confuse the viewer.

For example, we are in the office of an attorney in Chicago. He is talking to a colleague about a will the firm must execute, and he wonders where he can find a son who has not been heard from for many years. The next shot the writer wants to show is the son, in the kitchen of his ranch house in Arizona. But if we cut from the attorney's office to the young man at the kitchen table, the audience will have no idea where that table is (beyond perhaps guessing it may be somewhere in Chicago). The script writer, aware of this problem, provides a shot, or sometimes a series of shots, to clearly orient the viewer. In this case, since the change of locale is substantial, two establishing shots are warranted. The sequence might be: (1) attorney in Chicago office; (2) wide shot of cattle ranch; (3) close exterior shot of the ranch house and surrounding yard; (4) shot of young man at kitchen table.

Sometimes the details of the establishing shot are important, as in our specifying what kind of ranch it was (cattle); for story reasons it could have been even more specific, such as describing the ranch as huge, small, prosperous, dilapidated, etc. In such cases the script writer generally indicates the shot without labeling it as "establishing," since its purpose will be well understood.

When the writer is not interested in the details of the shot, only in its function, the script may then simply call for ESTABLISHING SHOT - RANCH, or ESTABLISHING SHOT - DOWNTOWN AREA.

The "lasting effect" of an establishing shot depends on how often the established scene recurs in the story. If we are to see our young rancher frequently, we can change at any time from Chicago, China or anywhere else, even to a closeup of him, and the audience will know where he is. But if the locale reappears only a few times, and separated each time by many other scenes, it should be briefly re-established whenever it is seen.

While establishing shots primarily are utilitarian, they can be used quite creatively by purposely delaying them. For example, a scene opens on a close shot of a man in a sun helmet staring fearlessly into the face of a nearby lion, against a backdrop of tropical foliage. A brave hunter in danger in the jungle—until the shot is widened to establish (or in this case, reveal) that the lion is in the corner of a cage, and the man is a zoo attendant, visiting the cage for his regular pickup.

*POV Shot*   POV is an abbreviation indicating that the viewer, via the camera, sees something from a specific Point Of View, almost always that of some person.

INT. MANHATTAN APARTMENT - DAY

Toni stands by a window, looking out. Noticing something on the street below, she smiles and waves her hand.

Milo, on the sidewalk below, smiles up at her as he
enters the building.

POV shots can make a point even when associated with
someone completely anonymous. For example, a character in
the story, a beautiful and shapely young woman, is walking
on a crowded beach, wearing a skimpy and revealing swim suit.
She passes a blanket on which a young man is sitting; he notices
her. Cut to the young man's POV as "his" glance lingers on
what she is displaying as she goes by. Although the young man's
role is but a walk-on (or, in this case, a sit-on) and he will
never be seen again, his POV shot conveys the point the writer
wants to make about the girl's walk.

POV shots are usually brief, but one notable POV sequence
lasted for an hour and forty-three minutes. The 1946 movie
*Lady in the Lake,* based on one of Raymond Chandler's private
eye stories, was filmed *entirely* from the point of view of the
main character. Everything is seen through his eyes, and the
audience only catches a fleeting glimpse of what he looks like
when he walks past the mirror of a vending machine. Robert
Montgomery, who directed, was billed as the star, but except
for his voice the leading role was actually played by a 35mm
camera.

*Reverse Angle Shot*   As the name indicates, a reverse angle
shot shows a 180° switch in the camera's view from the immediately preceding shot. A familiar example shows a visitor in an
apartment house corridor. He rings the doorbell of one apartment. The door opens, revealing the resident in the doorway.
REVERSE ANGLE—and we are now inside the apartment, looking out at the visitor in the doorway.

*The Closeup*   CU, the usual indication for a closeup shot
in a script, generally is interpreted by directors and camera
operators to mean a shot framing a subject's head; but the
term is relative enough so that some others will loosen the

shot to include part of the neck and shoulders, and still others may go close enough to show only the eyes and mouth.

Anything closer, such as the eyes or mouth alone, becomes an "extreme closeup," which is often abbreviated as ECU or XCU. Extreme closeups can be effective, but if shown *suddenly* they can be momentarily confusing, since something that we are used to always seeing as small now fills the entire screen. (One of the most startling ECU's ever used was a shot of Ray Milland's bleary right eyeball, from only six inches away, in the 1945 movie *The Lost Weekend*.)

It is possible to get into a discussion of "medium" close-ups, but the very term reflects the absence of precision as to what is wanted, and therefore it imparts uncertainty, rather than direction, when used in a script. When the effect of a close shot is wanted, but not a closeup, the best practice is simply to *call* it a CLOSE SHOT. Most professional scripts abound with directions such as:

CLOSE – HENRY

and let the director take it from there.

*Angle Shots*    There may be times when the writer envisions a particular dramatic effect to be gained by shooting from either a low angle or a high angle. People tend to assume an air of importance when they "loom" in a LOW ANGLE SHOT (General Douglas MacArthur reportedly seldom permitted any other kind of shot of himself). With the right shadow-lighting, the same shot can also contribute a sense of "menace" to a character.

A low angle shot can go just so low before the camera operator's chin touches the floor, but only the script writer knows how "high" a HIGH ANGLE SHOT should be, and therefore it requires a bit of guidance when used, as:

HIGH ANGLE SHOT

We see the entire basketball court, as from an upper-
tier seat.

     A HIGH ANGLE SHOT is presumed to be from a station-
ary position. If the camera is to shoot from a high angle while
moving, it will be mounted on a special crane:

CRANE SHOT

rising higher and higher, to reveal the broad spectrum
of activity on the busy street.

     The camera direction ANGLE appears alone quite fre-
quently in the typical script. It refers to changing to a new,
but unspecified, camera angle. Sometimes this is to "visually
punctuate" dialogue in a scene:

              JOHN
           You know I'm always
           there when you need me.

              DONNA
           Almost always.

ANGLE

John looks at Donna for a long moment before he
speaks.

              JOHN
           I thought we agreed never
           to mention that again.

     The "angle" could be a shot of John alone, or a shot of
both of them; but while the writer feels the need for a change
of angle at that point, it is left to the director to decide exactly
which angle the new one should be.
     Another example of leaving the choice to the director,
this time with no dialogue involved, would be:

Beverly hurries out of the phone booth.

ANGLE

to show her frantically looking around, not knowing in which direction to run.

*Stock Shot* A stock shot is nothing the camera does, but rather something the production goes out and rents. It refers to footage previously shot by someone else, and now part of the stock of a commercial film library. Shots of the New York skyline or the Golden Gate Bridge are examples of specific stock shots. Others, more generic, would be "a small-town Main Street," "a wide beach with palm trees" or "a busy downtown intersection." They are cannibalized from old movies, newsreels, travelogues, etc. If there is a shot in your movie or teleplay that has no dialogue or identifiable characters, you may see it five years from now as a stock shot in someone else's production. (Although the producer profits from this, the writer does not.)

It usually appears as:

EXT. BUSY AIRPORT - DAY (STOCK)

or more specifically:

INT. DULLES INTERNATIONAL AIRPORT - DAY (STOCK)

*Miscellaneous Shots*

*Long shot.* Usually seen as L.S., the long shot is occasionally further specified as MEDIUM LONG SHOT (M.L.S.) or EXTREME LONG SHOT (E.L.S. or X.L.S.).

*Single-shot, etc.* In a script SINGLE-SHOT - CHARLIE not only indicates that Charlie should be isolated by the camera, but that all or most of him will be seen (otherwise a CLOSE SHOT is indicated). The same applies to a TWO-SHOT, and possibly a THREE-SHOT, but beyond this grouping a script would more likely call for something like WIDE SHOT - THE FIVE BROTHERS.

*Tight shot.* The term *tight* indicates that the subject should fill the screen, as TIGHT ON TELEPHONE, etc. A tight shot is the cousin of a closeup.

*Full shot.* A full shot is specified when the writer has a special reason for wanting all parts of a person or object to be seen in the shot, and feels that in a *tight shot* or *single-shot* something might be left out.

In dealing with the *moving* shots of the camera, we are in a more interesting but somewhat trickier area. Camera moves contribute a depth of reality to a scene, *but every time an operating camera is moved, it involves one or more of the physical laws governing optics.* Camera operators, therefore, are like motorists going through a street heavily filled with traffic signs: they want to move to where they are going, but without violating any laws.

*Pan* When the camera in motion swings from left to right, or vice versa, it is *panning* (the word *pan* is a shortening of "panoramic shot," now seldom heard). The functional use of a pan is to follow someone or something moving laterally, or to fully reveal something wide. But it can have more creative uses when it makes a meaningful statement of its own.

One subtle example is a woman sitting next to her unattractive and irksome husband in their car. As it stops for a light, the woman sees a handsome and appealing man in the next car. A shot of the woman looking, then a separate shot of the man she sees, would "tell the story." But a continuous pan from her "looking" to him "being looked at" establishes the situation with more impact, since it lets the audience "share" her look by doing it with her.

There are two technical factors involved in panning. One is that the pan must be smooth, for the slightest shakiness will be magnified on the screen. The second, and by far the most important, is that pans must be relatively slow rather than fast.

Here the physics of the lens and the physiology of the eye combine in a complex way that involves the basic illusion of "moving pictures." If the pan is much too fast the shot will simply be blurred; but if the pan moves faster than a certain rate, yet not fast enough to blur, a phenomenon known as the stroboscopic effect (familiarly called "strobing") causes the frames of picture to be seen more as the series of still pictures they really are.

What it all means to the script writer is this: since the difference between fast and "too fast" in a pan is a tricky business to determine, be careful in calling for VERY FAST PAN. (You probably won't get it; if you get it you probably won't like it; if you do get it and like it, it probably will be technically more trouble than it was worth.)

*Tilt*   A camera does *not* "pan" up and down. The proper term for vertical movement of the camera is *tilt*. The camera pans the line of soldiers. It tilts up the church to show the steeple. Using the word *pan* for a tilt shot is one of the most common errors made by people on the periphery of film and television production (and by quite a few who are closer to the cameras).

A tilt is by no means merely the vertical equivalent of the pan, for the effect it can contribute, and the optical laws which come into play, are different. A tilting camera tends to distort the perspective of any subject close to it. But this very potential for distortion often is used creatively. The low angle shot which provided the "importance" or "menace" on a previous page was a tilt shot, although a stationary one. And many a modest-sized office building has loomed in an establishing shot as an imposing skyscraper, thanks to the camera tilting up from street to roof at a close-in angle.

*Dolly Shots*   So far we have seen the camera being moved up, down and sideways, but always while its tripod or base remained in one place. When the camera truly moves about, it is *dollying.* The name refers to the wheeled conveyance, or dolly, on which a film camera is often mounted. (Television cameras need no special gear when they dolly, since they normally ride on permanent wheeled pedestals.) A dolly for a film camera can be as small as a child's wagon or large enough to be motorized and driven.

The dolly shot is sometimes called different names, depending on what and how the camera shoots while on wheels. The dolly shot may also be called a *trucking shot.* When the camera follows and keeps pace with a subject it may be called a *tracking shot;* if the subject is moving along in a car or on horseback, it may be called a *traveling shot.*

When, instead of following a subject, it approaches or retreats, it is said to *dolly in* or *dolly out:*

DOLLY IN on a corner table, where Steve is finishing a lavish meal.

When it dollies in or out, the camera is subject to the optical law requiring that whenever the distance changes significantly between camera and subject the camera must be refocused. With a still photographer, who merely takes a few steps toward the subject, this is a simple chore. But a dollying camera is *continuously* changing its distance from its subject, and so each filmed dolly shot is carefully planned by the cinematographer; he or she (or an assistant) appropriately changes the focus on the camera during the shot. The TV camera operator does the same while dollying.

While DOLLY IN, DOLLY BACK, etc. will sometimes be seen in professional scripts, the terms are used on the set more than at the typewriter. Except when they feel such specificity is useful in communicating what they have in mind, most professional script writers simply tell the camera to "move," as in:

```
MOVE IN for tight shot of the red light as it flashes
on the control panel.
```

*The Zoom*    The key fact about the zoom is that it is an illusion. It is not, in fact, a *move* at all, but rather a photographic enlargement; because it is made before our eyes, it gives the *impression* that we have seen a move.

The special zoom lens, temporarily put on the camera, has many advantages, including the fact that it lets the camera seem to move toward objects which are physically inaccessible. The most notable feature, of course, is the familiar *z-o-o-m*, which is more dramatic than mere dollying.

Why, then, would you ever want to bother with a dolly shot? Because, except for those few times when you desire that vivid zoom effect, what you want is a bona fide *move*. To illustrate the difference, let us set our scene in a church, where a wedding is taking place. Our camera is on the center aisle, at the rear. The shot we want is a slow move down the aisle toward the wedding party in front of the clergyman.

If we make the shot using a camera mounted on a dolly, the camera will roll down the aisle, and the viewer will share the reality of the move as the camera passes nearby things—a pew ... another pew ... another pew in which a guest turns to speak to her companion ... past the best man ... ending in a close shot of the bridal couple.

Now let us make the same shot using a zoom lens. The camera remains in its position at the back door, and as the operator slowly cranks the zoom we see the bridal couple occupying more and more of the screen (being "enlarged") until they fill the screen completely. We get close to the couple, but we do *not* have the impression of really moving toward them; instead, they come toward us, in a kind of visual tunnel.

# SHOT AND SCENE TRANSITIONS

When a script writer indicates CUT TO, FADE OUT or any other transition, it does not really relate to the camera. In television these things are done in the control room, and in film they happen during the editing process after shooting is completed. Before we discuss their creative uses, let us see how they are accomplished technically.

*Cuts*  Cutting from one shot to another, or from one scene to the following, is the simplest transition. In television, the director merely gives instructions for a switch from one camera to another. The red light on one camera goes off, the red light on another camera goes on, and the cut from one angle to another is made (on the air, if it is live television).

In film, the director's command, "Cut!", may stop the cameras, but it is the film editor, later, who actually handles a blade. In a special film-cutting device, he or she cuts the film at the point chosen as the end of that shot, and splices it to the piece of film containing the next chosen shot. Since the last frame of one shot is immediately followed by the first frame of the next shot, the result is the abrupt change of the *cut.*

*Dissolve*  When the television director calls for a dissolve from one camera to another, the technical director nearby in the control room pushes two levers, which fade out the scene being shot by one camera while fading in what is being shot by the second camera. The incoming and outgoing scenes overlapping on the screen provides the appearance of a dissolve. By controlling how fast the levers are pushed the technical director can vary the length (or the speed) of any dissolve, depending on its desired dramatic effect.

The film editor does physically what the television control board does electronically. Deciding on the length of the dissolve (one-third of a second is a short one, two seconds is normal, three seconds is lingering), the film editor marks the film to indicate exactly which frames will overlap on the screen, and the negative is later shot accordingly.

*Fades*    In both film and television, a fade out is really a dissolve, but in this case to "black" (or sometimes "white") instead of to another shot or scene.

*Wipes*    The most familiar wipe shows the incoming scene arriving from the left and "wiping away" the existing scene. However, the arriving scene can come from any portion of the screen, and may even start to appear in fragments which form into the new scene.

Wipes are accomplished on film by using mattes which blot out parts of scenes and then insert others to replace them, all of which is done in a system of shooting and over-shooting by a special camera designed for this purpose.

Television accomplishes the same thing by an electronic process of its own, which integrates parts of scenes, fed from various sources into a central bank of circuits, and arranges them into desired form on the screen (or on the videotape).

The more interesting a wipe is, the more expensive it usually is to produce, especially on film.

*Swish Pan*    Cuts, dissolves, fades and wipes are the work-horses among transitional devices, but a device once used only rarely has now become popular: the *swish pan.* As its name quite vividly indicates, it is an extremely fast pan. You will recall that if a pan is made too rapidly the result will be a blur. In this case, the blur is on purpose, to capture the effect of an almost hallucinogenic whirl of colored or white lights. While any production that is in the shooting stage can make one, many film editors keep a supply of ready-made swish pans.

*The Creative Use of Transitions*    Fashions in screen transitions change. At one time, earlier in filmmaking (and before television), it was more or less understood among directors and film editors that cuts, dissolves and fades between scenes generally related to the passage of screen time. Cuts were usually used between the shots within a scene. The dissolve was the doorway to the next scene, as well as the indicator that time had passed. Fading out and fading in indicated a major passage of time, or the close of a key segment in the story.

Today much of that has changed. In many movies and teleplays it seems that almost every scene cuts to the next scene. This sometimes causes momentary confusion, when there is no continuity between the last thing we see in one scene and the first thing we suddenly see in the new scene. While this may be outweighed by the brisk pace a particular movie or teleplay has as a result of *cut, cut, cut* between every scene, not every story warrants a brisk pace. An otherwise well-written and well-acted production can be marred because its dramatic tempo—a vital element in any screen story—is inappropriate.

The important point for the script writer to understand is that transitional devices affect the pace and tempo of a movie or teleplay, and thus should not be casually written in. When you want to indicate what you strongly believe a transition should be—perhaps a series of quick cuts or a lingering dissolve—you certainly should make your meaning known. Most other times, let the editor edit.

## SPECIAL EFFECTS

In both film and videotape production the gamut of possible special effects is nearly unlimited, ranging from interesting to mind-boggling. Ever since the public first started to see special effects in movies—objects being carried by invisible people, actors standing next to themselves, etc.—they have been called "camera tricks." But, in fact, they seldom originate in the camera. Rather, they are the result of complex, expensive processes which are frequently more interesting than the shows in which they are used.

There are two kinds of special effects. One is the simulation. An example of this is shooting a small model of a ship in a vat of water; later on the screen it would be seen as the ship in the story being dashed about, and possibly destroyed, by "giant" waves (which actually reach the awesome height of three or four inches). Other special effects of this type include using carefully controlled jets of flame in a "burning" room or wind machines creating "typhoons" or "desert sandstorms."

However, the kind of special effect most often used, which we will examine, is not done with simulation equipment on a rigged set, but rather less spectacularly via post-production techniques.

In film production they are called *optical effects* (or simply *opticals*). After filming is completed, they generally are accomplished in a series of steps by a special system of camera lenses at a commercial studio specializing in these effects. (It is here that our scene transitions are made, for they too are opticals.) In television the complex circuitry which makes most special effects possible may be used right in the control room (or nearby) while the cameras are shooting, although it is often done later during videotape editing.

Special effects can dazzle. That is why television commercials, written in glib, catchy phrases which convey thin concepts, are often loaded with lots of effects, to hide the fact that no really significant thoughts are being communicated. But since movies and teleplays are written in meaningful words, comprising bona fide communication, the typical script (not written for a science fiction extravaganza) contains few if any effects. When they do, it is usually one of the following.

*Process Shot*   The most commonly used special effect is a shot using process photography: live action in the foreground combined with a filmed scene in the background. This is done with a special projector that works from behind a screen rather than in front of it (known as *rear projection,* or simply R.P.). A man and woman are standing on a bluff; behind them we see Niagara Falls. Actually they are in the corner of a studio, standing before an R.P. screen. In the movie or teleplay, after the roar of the falls has been dubbed in, the audience will practically see the misty spray falling on the couple.

Process shots are frequently used for scenes actually shot in a studio but supposedly taking place inside a moving car—

```
INT. JACK'S CAR - DAY (PROCESS)
```

with the rear projection screen being seen through the car's back window, showing a stock shot of moving traffic.

*Split Screen*   Although the screen can be split into many segments, each containing a different scene, the typical split screen shows only two, often the two ends of a telephone conversation. For example, we are in the living room of Vic and Jody's home. She answers the phone:

```
                JODY
    Oh hello, Vic. Where are you?

SPLIT SCREEN: VIC IN STREET PHONE BOOTH

                VIC
    I had a flat tire.
```

*Freeze Frame*   "Freezing," or suspending, the action is a device sometimes used by script writers or directors to highlight some dramatic point, such as the look on someone's face as they react. When used this way, freeze frames tend to disrupt the flow of a scene unless they occur on the last shot. Moreover, they have greatest impact when they are followed not by a cut or dissolve, but by a fade out. Therefore, in a teleplay, the best place to put one is on the last shot of a scene that ends an act.

Freeze frames should really not be expected to last more than a few seconds. This is because individual frames of film and videotape are not as sharp as still photographs, and while this is never apparent when the frames go by at their normal twenty-four per second in film and thirty per second in tape, it becomes noticeable when a single frame lingers for inspection.

*Montage*  A screen montage is a series of brief scenes, often without dialogue, separated by slowly overlapping dissolves. It is meant to show a related sequence of actions, or the passing of time. If more than one scene is on the screen at the same time it is a special effect.

John, just out of prison, has promised his wife he will work hard at his new job at the steel mill. Then the following brief scenes:

1. John punching in at the time clock.
2. John carrying a large burden up a flight of stairs.
3. John getting dirty as he cleans a grease pit.
4. John being patted on the shoulder by the boss.

This device (and often with scenes of this kind) was very common in movies of the thirties and forties. Today it is seldom used, except occasionally as an impressionistic statement by directors whose films are more reflections of a mood than a story.

I think the traditional montage has fallen out of use because it gives the impression of being a shortcut in writing the script. This may have been more acceptable back when Hollywood screenwriters had to turn out a product on a factory schedule, but not in today's smaller and more competitive market for quality scripts.

*Slow Motion*  Using slow motion to establish a dream sequence is something of a cliché. On its way to becoming one is using slow motion to extend some violent action, which if played at normal speed would happen too fast for the audience to see in detail. Sudden disasters such as train wrecks, and scenes wherein someone bursts into a room and riddles the occupants with machine gun bullets, often are shown at sloweddown speed for the audience to fully appreciate.

Ordinarily, slow motion is quite simple to accomplish: the film camera merely shoots the scene at a faster speed than normal; then, when played back at standard speed, the action appears as the familiar slow motion. In videotape it is done electronically in or near the control room by a special Slow Motion Disk, nicknamed "Slomo," a sophisticated relative of the video disk.

But variations can sometimes be more complicated. Many years ago, I had the idea to have everyone in a scene except the principal character move in slow motion. This, I found, required an extremely complex process called a traveling matte, and in opticals, "complex" means "expensive"—in this case much too expensive for my modest budget at that time. But the same thing could happen with a multi-million-dollar feature film budget. The wise writer never inextricably implants some unusual effect in a script *before* its potential cost has been determined. A prospective producer may decide that it is more expensive than the effect of the effect is worth.

*Camera shots, film and television production techniques—is it necessary to know something about all this in order to be a script writer? Frankly, no. But it is necessary in order to be a good script writer—and indispensable to being a great one.*

*It was said earlier that scripts of the best movie and television writers contain few camera directions because what the camera will do is often implicit in the way they write their scenes. But how could they think and write cinematically unless they knew these camera directions, and understood what they represent?*

*Writing for film and television means writing in the conceptual terms of these media, which are weddings of art and technology. The more you know of the technology, the better you can practice your art.*

# 8
# Packaging
# and Selling
# Your Script

You cannot make any money writing movie or television scripts. The money comes from *selling* your scripts.

Even setting aside the realities of the marketplace (both the one for scripts and the one where you buy your groceries), the writer of an unproduced script cannot enjoy the satisfaction possible to the writer of an unpublished prose work. For the prose writer can show the completed, but unsold, manuscript to his or her friends, and except for lacking a binding, it can be read and admired exactly as though it were published. But the screenplay or teleplay is not written to be read. It is a literary Sleeping Beauty—waiting for the kiss of the camera to bring it to life.

Therefore, it does not matter whether the script writer's prime motive is money or artistic satisfaction, or both; neither one can be realized unless the script is bought (or commissioned) by a producer. With this as a goal, the writer must do three things: package the script, protect the script (and its writer) and then market the script.

The writer is naturally more interested in the script's contents than in its wrapper. But while the contents *is* the script, the mundane considerations of its physical appearance should never be depreciated—not only out of pride, but also for a more practical reason.

116

Producers, story editors, agents—in fact, anyone routinely handling professional scripts—are accustomed to seeing them impeccably typed and crisply neat. This is simply because the typical professional script circulating in the industry will have been prepared by one of the many script-service establishments on which almost everyone working on or with a script relies. This means that a script's slightest sloppiness, or its not being bound in some kind of cover, can go a long way as a reminder that it was written by a beginner.

There are two areas of protection the script writer should consider: protection of his or her property, and personal protection against legal problems arising out of what appears on the screen as a result of the script. (The protection of literary property, and of its authors, are complex matters and the subject of many books. What is offered here is merely general discussion, with any advice coming not from an attorney but from a professional writer.)

What many beginning writers may not fully realize is that the *story* inherent in an original screenplay or teleplay is a separate property. The higher fee for an original script, not based on someone else's story, reflects this. Thus when you protect your script you are also protecting the equally valuable story it contains. Indeed, many professional script writers take steps to protect their stories even before they plan the scripts which will eventually be based on them.

Sending yourself a script, outline or synopsis by certified mail and not opening the sealed envelope is a simple procedure. This establishes a specific date which you may be able to use in claiming you had the idea first. But one disadvantage of this form of protection is that it provides no conventional way of noting what you have done on the title page of the script. A notice such as SENT TO SELF VIA CERTIFIED MAIL & UNOPENED is certainly possible—but it is cumbersome, to say the very least. So that your script may bear some amulet to ward off any potential poacher, there are two alternatives:

copyright, or registry with the Writers Guild. (Titles, either alone or when part of a literary work, are not protected by copyright or Guild registry.)

To obtain copyright protection for an original motion picture screenplay or teleplay, request an application for Class D (dramatic compositions) from:

> Register of Copyrights
> Library of Congress
> Washington, D.C. 20540

The Writers Guild of America has a registration service to assist its members in establishing the identity and completion date of their work. However, the service is also available to nonmembers, who may then note "Registered with WGA" on their title pages. The fee is nominal and the registration is valid for ten years and renewable. The Writers Guild is two affiliated unions, East and West. Both accept material in completed script form as well as synopses, outlines, treatments or story ideas. Details of the service, and the registration envelopes required, may be obtained by writing:

> Writers Guild of America, East
> 555 West 57th Street
> New York, N.Y. 10019

> or

> Writers Guild of America, West
> 8955 Beverly Boulevard
> Los Angeles, Calif. 90048

Just as important as protecting your own property is making sure that you do not inadvertently poach somebody else's material. Generally, you may not use any coprighted material without authorization. It is true that there is a so-called "fair use" doctrine, sometimes making it possible to use quotations without specific permission of the copyright holder. But this is an area open to inconclusive interpretation, and it is sometimes more trouble to risk unauthorized "fair use" than to get written permission.

Most people are aware that material not copyrighted is in the public domain, but this sometimes misleads even the most experienced writers. Take the trouble to check for copyright of the specific version on which you plan to base a script. The fact that the author of a story has been dead for two hundred years or more does not always mean that *this translation,* or *this particular version,* is not copyrighted by someone.

Another possible area of unexpected trouble concerns real people portrayed on the screen without their prior consent. In the case of famous people, the producer will probably make a judgment about potential problems. It is the nonfamous real people whom the script writer should worry about.

If you create a totally fictitious character named Zebia, who has one arm and cheats his customers at his grocery store, you may hear from just such a real person, claiming you slandered him. Proving you never heard of him, if you can, may possibly end the matter. But what if you decide to be "clever" and purposely pattern the licentious insurance agent in your script after the licentious insurance agent on your street? The real one may be named Smith, and your scripted one may be named Klopfenhopper—but you are still in trouble. He may be able to show that his *personality,* if not his name, was used.

Legally, the script writer has some chance of successfully defending against a claim that his or her material defamed or invaded the privacy of any person if it cannot be shown that ". . . the writer *knowingly* used the name or personality of such person, or *should have known* in the exercise of reasonable prudence, that such person would or might claim that his personality was used in such material."

There is one other area in which the script writer, and most particularly the beginner, often needs protection, and this is in dealing with those who buy his or her scripts. The making of movies and television programs are major industries, and the details of the business relationship between producers and script writers are complex. Specifying and governing these details is the Basic Agreement between the Writers Guild of America, to which almost all writers for American movies and television belong, and members of the Association of Motion Picture and Television Producers.

This document, running to well over two hundred pages, is the basis for contracts between writers and producers, and in it, all issues affecting the professional writing and selling of scripts are clearly defined and agreed upon. For example, it defines and sets fees for every step of the script process: story idea, outline, treatment and screenplay or teleplay (and it differentiates between a "rewrite" and a "polish"). In addition, it covers a myriad of other matters, from screen credits to "reading time" for scripts under consideration.

Membership in the Writers Guild is open to new members at WGA East or West, based on which side of the Mississippi River they reside.

Any discussion about making that crucial first script sale should realistically include "without wasting time, effort and hope." With that in mind, let us examine the script markets, and how to sell to them.

The market for scripts of theatre movies is smaller and more restricted than that for television scripts, but it is much richer, since the minimum fees are higher (and few screenwriters receive the minimum). There may be two or three hundred feature films seen in theatres each year. Some of these are foreign and others are produced by independent producers who may turn out one picture every few years.

The six major Hollywood studios—Universal, 20th Century-Fox, Paramount, M-G-M/UA, Warner Brothers and Columbia—are collectively responsible for about a hundred pictures each year, which they partly finance and/or distribute and/or help to produce. Their output is where the regular, more predictable activity is centered.

The typical movie deal is a marvel of complexity, and only

about 10 percent of all movie projects started and developed ever reach the production stage. The other 90 percent are canceled at some point along the way, but sometimes they are picked up by others, who also may or may not take the property to the final stage of production and release. Thus the odds are 10-to-1 that your "first sale" may turn out to be only your "first option." But while this is disappointing, it does mean that you were paid something. Many screenwriters derive surprising amounts of option money from screenplays considered and returned by a number of producers.

Between 30 and 40 percent of all movies produced in an average year are adaptations of books or plays. For obvious reasons, a producer would rather pay a fortune for screen rights to a best seller than a few thousand for an original screenplay by a relative unknown. This is balanced somewhat by the fact that some producers do not have access to any fortune, but *can* scrape up the Guild minimum which will attract only an unknown's screenplay.

In television having an agent is desirable, but in theatrical movies it is just about essential. There are story editors at the major studios, and at the offices of the more active and successful independent producers—but they primarily spend their time in considering books which are not yet published, some of which are submitted and some of which they seek out. Realistically, the only original screenplays seriously considered (or even taken out of their envelopes by some story editors or producers) are those from established agents.

The fledgling script writer who starts to probe the market by sending material to likely outlets soon learns about the barrier against unsolicited scripts. Scripts often come back unopened, and letters of inquiry are answered by terse announcements of policy about "unsolicited material" or "dealing only through established agents."

This apparent disinterest is discouraging. While I can only sympathize with the discouragement, I can clarify the motivation behind what causes it. It is seldom simply disinterest, but fear. This is not the same fear that may inspire so many decisions in television. Most movie and television organizations, large and small, make a company policy out of xenophobia; they are afraid of strangers. They are wary of relations with people outside the profession because they are afraid of being sued for "stealing" some amateur's story idea. There are, after all, just so many variations on so many basic plots. Their fear (often based on painful experience) is that somebody will see a show about a boy and his dog aboard the first spaceship going to Mars, and "recognize" that as their story about a boy and his dog on grandfather's farm, which was politely rejected five years ago.

Many movie companies will not even send their release form, when requested, so that it could accompany unsolicited material. (Perhaps they're afraid of being accused of stealing your idea for how to word a release form.)

An agent's imprint on a script, however, can take the sting out of an unfamiliar name below the title. Besides this advantage, of course, agents are in a position to know and frequently see the people who buy and commission scripts.

Getting an agent is not impossible, but neither is it simple. Ironically, the more desirable an agent is from your point of view (that is, the more easily he or she can make a sale with a telephone call), the less they are interested in handling a writer who is not already earning large sums. Thus it is often a waste of time to try to get a large, busy agency (or a very busy and successful individual agent) to take you on as a client. But even if you could, that too could be a waste of time, because you might very well languish unsold while they concentrated on their more lucrative clients, or relegated your account to their most inexperienced staff agent, recently out of the mail room.

The best kind of agent to have when you are a beginning writer is one small enough to be motivated to develop and sell your work, yet established enough to be able to do it.

Not all literary agents are engaged in handling scripts; many confine their activities to the publishing world. Among agents who do have script writers as clients, the great majority are in the Los Angeles area, about forty are in New York City (many with branches or correspondent agents on the west coast) and about twenty more are scattered throughout the rest of the country. You may obtain a list of agents who represent script writers from the Writers Guild. It is particularly useful because it notes which of the agents have agreed to consider the work of novices.

You should send the prospective agent a completed screenplay, not a story idea or an outline. If you have more than one completed movie script which you feel shows merit, send them all (*always* keeping a carbon or photocopy). Even if he or she does not send them out, they will help to provide the agent with a better idea of your potential.

Your first sale, however, will probably be to television. While it is not easy in either media, it is *comparatively* easier to sell a script to television only because that market needs and consumes so many more of them.

In the average commercial network season, there may be between forty-five and sixty dramatic or comedy programs, depending upon each network's proportion of hour and half-hour shows at the time. Most probably, however, about 40 percent will be half-hour programs, which almost always means comedies.

Approximately 15 percent of the programs will be "closed"—either staff-written (which is rare) or, more usually, divided among a small group of selected free-lance writers contracted to provide all the scripts for that program. The rest will be "open."

In addition, there are usually six to eight movie nights, which frequently play made-for-TV movies that are really two-hour teleplays. An occasional two-hour dramatic special may be aired in a nonmovie time period, pre-empting the regularly scheduled programs. (This is a mixed blessing for script writers: one writer gets a huge fee for a TV-movie, and two to four others miss out on writing scripts for the programs which are dislodged that night.)

Thus, besides TV-movies, mini series, non-network shows in first-run syndication, and made-for-cable series, there are usually about forty network programs that are open to free-lance writers. The question is, which free-lance writers?

The largest group includes those who live in the Los Angeles area. It is, in fact, only by living there and having an agent that a writer can hope to earn the large income possible from *regularly* writing for the network programs. These writers are readily available for story conferences, sudden changes, last-minute assignments.

The next largest group (but only relatively, for it is by no means large) consists of writers who do not live in or near Los Angeles, but whose agents do. The agents sell their "unsolicited" scripts, and get them assignments to write others. When necessary, the writers fly in to do some writing, or to be available for conferences and revisions until the script is "locked." (If their agent is one of those not in Los Angeles, or at least New York, they probably write and sell more so-called long-form scripts than for the one-hour or half-hour series, since the latter require much closer market contact on the agent's part.)

The last group may be found anywhere in the country— but without an agent. This group does not sell a lot of scripts, but they do sell some.

What can you do to sell that first script on your own?

The most realistic first goal is one of the hour-long or half-hour series. This invites a producer to take less of a chance in buying an unknown's script than with a TV-movie or multi-night "miniseries."

A vital factor in selling television scripts is having access to basic production information:

1. What shows are being produced and are open for scripts?
2. What kind of scripts are required?
3. Whose shows are they?
4. Where is production being done?
5. Who are the story editors?
6. Are the shows on film or videotape?

As a writer-seller of television scripts, you do not care which network is involved, who the individual producer or director may be, or the scheduled air time of the show. You need only these six facts.

If necessary, you can learn all of them, except receptivity to outside scripts, by simply watching any show that is already on the air. The production companies involved are always identified as the very last items of the closing credits. The story editor (not to be confused with similar titles such as *story consultant* or *script consultant*) will receive prominent screen credit. And if it is not a half-hour comedy, in which somebody's voice usually announces "This program was filmed [taped] before a live audience," a sharp eye will see a credit either for *film editor* or *videotape editor* among the multiple credits at the end.

This method of obtaining basic production information is readily available, and has all the virtues of any do-it-yourself project. However, besides not knowing if the show is open or closed to outside scripts, you have no way of knowing whether the show's script-buying period is over, or if they buy outside scripts on assignment only, or other facts which would make it a waste of time to offer your work.

Writers' magazines frequently carry the needed information. In addition, there is a booklet called *Ross Reports,* generally unknown outside the television industry, which gives useful script market and production information about all network television series (including new ones about to be produced), with relevant names and addresses. It is sold by monthly subscription, but you may obtain one by single-copy sale from Television Index, Inc., 150 Fifth Avenue, New York, N.Y. 10011.

The program for which you want to write a script may be one you have seen many times, but now you should not only watch it, but study it. Are there any previously unnoticed subtleties in the relationships of the regular characters? Is there a discernible pattern to how each story opens, or approaches a break, or closes? Analyze it, not as a viewer but as a *writer.*

What you send the story editor should not be a story idea

or an outline. Established writers may submit an outline and then receive an assignment to write the script, but the extent of *your* ability to write a finished teleplay is not known to any story editor. Therefore a complete script (in the appropriate film or tape format) is a more logical first submission.

However, before you write it and send it off, consider the fact that even those story editors and producers who might be willing to read an unsolicited script will probably do so only after you have signed a release form.

In writing to request a release form, it is best to state your intent *but provide no glowing description of the proposed script.* Any advance disclosure about story or characters defeats the very purpose of a release form. If you have any professional writing credits, in any medium, mention them briefly. If not, academic or educational credentials may be provided if they are significant. (And enclosing a postage stamp as a courtesy is always a good idea.)

Some may never answer your letter. Others may cite the familiar policy about dealing only through agents. Still others may respond quite cordially, but only to tell you that the season's scripts are already committed, or asking to be told when something of yours is on the air in somebody else's show, or even revealing that the series has been canceled.

But it is also possible that, in the game of script roulette, your number will come up.

Unlike the movie dramatist, the television dramatist has an alternate market: public television.

There are almost three hundred public television stations in the country, with only a handful now engaged in any significant dramatic production. But although the market is small, it can be quite lucrative to the script writer, since script fees are often the same Writers Guild rates as in commercial television, but there are usually many more replays.

Teleplays are bought under a standard five-year contract, which provides for four releases in three consecutive years. (If the script remains unproduced three years from the date of its delivery, all rights revert to the author, who is free to sell it again elsewhere.)

While the sale of a script is a matter of dealing with an individual station, production on any station is often followed by telecasting on most of the other public television stations.

The major play-producing stations in public television are WNET, New York; WGBH, Boston; KCET, Los Angeles; KQED, San Francisco; and WQED, Pittsburgh.

*We have talked about script "markets" in the movies, the commercial networks and public television. But though a script is written to be sold, it is never just another product, for it comes, not out of its maker's hands, but from within its creator's mind and heart.*

*And so selling a script involves a great deal more than money—especially the first one. It is not the call of commerce that quickens the heartbeat of the beginning script writer who sees that an envelope has arrived from California—and it is small and white, not large and brown.*

# 9
# Specialized Writing
# for Film
# and Television

This book is primarily for the dramatist working in film and television, but there are other kinds of writers working in highly specialized areas of these media, mostly in salaried staff positions. These areas include:

- TV commercials and promos
- The TV interview or talk show
- The TV game show
- Soap operas
- Documentaries

More informational than instructional, our examination of these areas (and a miscellany of others) will center on what *kind* of writing is involved, and some of the considerations which affect it.

## TV COMMERCIALS AND PROMOS

A great deal of creativity goes into the writing and production of TV commercials (certainly far more than in many of the programs which carry them). But it is a very special kind of creativity. A TV commercial (like all basic advertising) is designed for one narrow purpose—moving products off store shelves.

The advertising agencies, where commercials are born, often make incredible sojourns into motivational psychology, demographics, market research minutiae, and an ever-widening scope of techniques for pre-testing commercials and products, ranging from monitoring volunteers' sweat glands to analyzing their brain waves.

The research forms the basis for a decision about what kind of advertising campaign is indicated. This, like much of the activity at an agency, is implemented as the effort of a creative team, of which the writer is a part. They are usually guided by a basic tenet of advertising: emphasize *the promise of a product* rather than its function. Thus the selling point of a soap is not the cleanliness it offers, but how that cleanliness may activate one's sex life.

TV commercial writing reflects the context in which the commercial is seen: its entire duration is a fleeting thirty seconds or less, and it appears as part of the clutter in a break. Consequenty, effective TV commercial writing consists of pungent word groups, meant to impart concepts rather than information, and simple enough to be grasped in a hurry.

On-air promos are close relatives of commercials. These are the brief trailers seen along with commercials in any break, promoting the programs of the network or the local station. They can be as simple as a few scenes excerpted from the show being promoted, or as elaborately written, produced and musically scored as any TV commercial. These are generally the handiwork of staff writer-producers in the advertising departments of the three networks and the larger local TV stations.

## THE TV INTERVIEW OR TALK SHOW

People generally do not think of television interview or talk shows as being "written." But television air time—especially network air time—is far too precious to be left to the vagaries of conversational chance. Different programs have different formats, depending on the style (and ability) of the host. However, they are generally variations on the following basic procedure.

When the guest is booked for an appearance, a "pre-interview" is arranged with a member of the program staff. Depending on the show's budget, this may be by a "reporter" who gathers the material on which the script will be based, or it may be part of the script writer's job.

In preparation for the pre-interview, the staff member does some research on the guest. In the case of an author, the reporter or script writer either reads or scans the book, noting areas which could be the basis for questions the host may ask on the air. In the case of stars who are on the talk show circuit to sell their latest movie or record, more creative research is necessary in seeking fertile grounds for questions.

At the pre-interview (often held in a hotel room or restaurant), the staff member asks dozens of questions suggested by the book or by the research material (which generally consists of old newspaper or magazine stories about the guest, or, if not famous, about the guest's field of activity).

The staff member makes notes of each answer. Most important of all, he or she notes which of the questions "play," that is, which ones evoke an interesting response, an unexpected answer or a colorful reaction.

Back at the program office, the script is written for that guest's segment of the show. All the questions that "played" are put at the top. If there were enough of them, the entire segment will consist of these questions. If there were only a few, they will be asked early in the hope that they may be stretched as long as possible. (If there were none, the writer may suggest that the producer consider canceling the guest.)

If done properly, the script will consist of each question followed in parentheses by a capsulization of the expected answer, so that the host may prod the guest to elicit a response if necessary. On the better shows, the producer or host will insist that the questions be not merely compiled and formulated, but written well enough to sound interesting and articulate.

On the air, if everything is working as it should (which

means the guest did not either refuse the pre-interview nor show up in an alcoholic glow), the segment is an interesting one, with the audience appreciating the interviewing or conversational skill of the host.

The screen credit of the writers sometimes depends on the ego of the host. Some talk show personalities are reluctant to list "writers" of a program which presumably is built around their conversational skill. Thus some writers' names may appear as part of a *Program Staff* credit on the screen. (When I wrote a celebrity-interview TV show on NBC a number of years ago, I had to be satisfied with the ambiguous screen credit for *Continuity*.)

## THE TV GAME SHOW

Writers on the staffs of game shows (which include quiz and audience participation programs) have perhaps the most specialized of all creative jobs in television. On some shows, much of the staff's effort is devoted to thinking up an endless variety of stunts, but on others they earn the designation of "writer" at their typewriters.

The questions on a quiz show that sound so simple are actually constructed according to a strict format. For example, "Who invented the sewing machine?" is not a good question, because the contestant can start thinking of a list of inventors upon hearing the second word. An experienced quiz show writer would instead start out with "Who discovered. . . ." Here the contestant has no idea if the discovery relates to a country, a movie star or a scientific principle. Thus there is no blurting out of an answer before the host has even completed the question. Instead, there can be a suspenseful pause between "Who discovered . . ." and ". . . radium?" (Or "Canada?")

Game shows on which the host regularly engages in entertaining banter with the guests may be fully scripted. Although many of these hosts are hired for their natural wit in the first place, the security of pre-written ad libs is often too tempting to resist.

For example, Johnny Carson, host of *The Tonight Show* for more than seventeen years, previously was host of a quiz show on ABC called *Who Do You Trust?* Carson has one of the readiest natural wits in the business. In addition, he is particularly skillful in eliciting entertaining responses from others. Despite this, the banter with his guests, which preceded the questions, was carefully scripted, and then rehearsed between the writers and the prospective contestants, sometimes down to every last "Oh, really?" (Apparently, to *Who Do You Trust?*, Carson's answer was, "The writers.")

## SOAP OPERAS

The writers of soap operas (more formally called *serials* in the industry) are television dramatists, but it is a specialized and atypical kind of drama, and the scripts are never bought on the open market.

If in other areas of screen drama a good rule is *show it, don't say it,* the rule in soap opera writing is *show it and say it . . . and say it . . . and say it.* There are, however, practical reasons for the leaden pace of soap operas, and also for the fact that the characters in them talk endlessly about what they plan to do, then about what they are doing, and even more about what they have done. The key is the traditional viewing pattern of a soap opera's audience.

Viewers generally are addicted to their favorite dramas, but since the shows are on every single day, it is inevitable that even the most firmly hooked "soap opera junkie" will miss an episode now and then. Since they are shown during the daytime, the exigencies of real life, on the viewer's side of the screen, often intervene. Sometimes this is only for a day or two, but often it is longer, such as at vacation time.

The way the scripts are written, if viewers are absorbed in Jessica's plan to poison Roger (for causing Larry's suicide after Fran's abortion), they can go away and come back days later to find they have not missed the poisoning which Jessica is still only talking about.

Another reason for the endless rehashing by the characters of how they feel and what they plan to do, or have done, is that it makes entry easy for new viewers, who thereby learn in their first episode most of the details of what is happening, and to whom.

Soap operas are noted for the throbbing sensationalism of their plots. Their characters' ordinary everyday lives are regularly filled with rape, murder, insanity, suicide, incest, blackmail and treason. One prime reason for this relates to how they are produced. The typical soap opera is videotaped on the same three or four sets inside a studio each day. Therefore, instead of things *happening*, in various locales, as in most prime time drama series, the action in a soap opera is primarily *talked about*—the viewer sees very little of it actually taking place. To avoid the pall that would fall over the viewer's interest after watching people talk for five days each week, that talk must be as titillating as possible.

## DOCUMENTARIES

Documentaries for television or theatre screens very seldom originate with a script writer, unless he or she is actually a producer-writer. The typical documentary is a producer's project, and the script is usually an adjunct element in which the writer's main creative contribution is the narration.

This is because of how most documentaries are made. Some contain only original footage; others combine stock footage, borrowed film clips and still photos. The typical documentary, however, is a combination of all these elements, any of which may prove impossible to obtain after being included in the advance planning. A writer, therefore, ordinarily cannot sit down and "write" a documentary, unless he or she has absolute knowledge of what visual content will accompany the narration. (While not usual, this is far from impossible; for example, a writer may conceive a documentary about the art works in a certain museum, or group of museums.)

No two documentaries are alike in the circumstances of their concept and in their production. Generally a preliminary outline is blocked out, to which the writer may or may not contribute. As production proceeds, the producer remains flexible, for usually it is found that certain planned shooting cannot be done, some stills or art work will not be available, and possibly some on-camera interviews have to be canceled. Thus, while the basic outline remains intact, the actual content of a documentary often changes as it is produced.

If the documentary has an on-camera narrator, speaking at various locations, the writer (usually hired on a free-lance basis) will be working on the production almost from the start. Where and how narration will be used is planned, but never completely certain until the end of shooting. A planned segment in which the narrator says, on the steps of the Capitol, "This is where much of the power is," may end up on the screen as a stock footage shot, with the line delivered voice-over.

The script may go into its first draft as soon as the documentary has been assembled on film or tape in rough form. Each scene is handled differently by the writer: some visually generic scenes will rely heavily on the narration; some will require only brief captioning; others will have no narration at all.

With variations depending on scope, subject and budget, many business and instructional films are written and produced in a similar way.

## MISCELLANEOUS TELEVISION WRITING

*Comedy-variety writing*   The writers of scripts for the half-hour comedy series are dramatists working in the comedy form. Another kind of comedy writing, often called gag writing, relates to the one-liners and brief comedy sketches in a weekly show or one-time special that has no story line. If the star or many of the guests are musical, it may be called a variety show rather than a comedy show. The difference simply means that in addition to gags for the comics, the writers will also script entertaining banter to be used by the musical acts.

*Light commentary*  An almost invisible but often essential script is one written for celebrities who act as hosts for the coverage of events such as nationally telecast parades or other spectacles. It consists of brief comments about what the camera is showing at the moment, as well as every word of the chit-chat exchanged between the co-hosts, or spoken by a host to the TV audience. These celebrities are hired for their name value, not their conversational skills, and they (and the producers) derive great comfort from the security afforded by the script. A few celebrities dislike having their every innocuous remark about the weather written down for them, and will make a point of occasionally departing from the script—except at key points, where particular words of their banter are prearranged cues for switching procedures all along the network before each commercial break.

*Some writers interested in movie or television drama might consider their kind of writing to be more meaningful than what is turned out by many of the specialized and often anonymous writers we have just discussed. Perhaps it is. But it is by no means more creative.*

*The traditional free-lance script writer is inspired to creativity when The Flash comes, the idea gels (or the spouse nags). But these other script writers must learn to be creative on demand, whether they feel "inspired" or not. I have been on both sides and I know. It is, in fact, not easy to sit down at a moment's notice and say, in Shakespeare's words, "Devise, wit; write, pen;" and do it.*

# Afterword

The closing is the traditional place for credits to roll, and so this farewell scene is an appropriate place for me to put one credit into perspective.

Throughout these pages I have counseled you to let the actor act, let the director direct, and so on, bidding you to be content to remain the script writer.

But bidding you to be content to remain the script writer on a production is asking you to be content to be some kind of god, for you *create* what all the others merely work on. I have heard many discussions about who is the most important factor in a movie or teleplay, and while we hear of "an Alfred Hitchcock film" or "a Marlon Brando vehicle," the bottom line that nobody has yet been able to refute is: If the writer hadn't written it, there wouldn't *be* anything to act in or direct in the first place.

In the legalistic Basic Agreement between the Writers Guild and the producers, amidst all the ponderous clauses, with their wherefores and hereinafters, appears the industry's officially accepted definition of a script writer: "A writer is a creative and professional person who performs a unique and indispensable function in relation to the production. . . ."

Unique and indispensable. Think of that when you put your script under your arm and set out to follow the yellow brick road.

FADE OUT.

THE END

# Index

# Index

# Index

# Index